French
ONE

FOR COMMON ENTRANCE

Nigel Pearce

GALORE PARK

AN HACHETTE UK COMPANY

Although every effort has been made to ensure that website addresses are correct at time of going to press, Galore Park cannot be held responsible for the content of any website mentioned in this book. It is sometimes possible to find a relocated web page by typing in the address of the home page for a website in the URL window of your browser.

Hachette UK's policy is to use papers that are natural, renewable and recyclable products and made from wood grown in sustainable forests. The logging and manufacturing processes are expected to conform to the environmental regulations of the country of origin.

Orders: **Teachers** please contact Bookpoint Ltd, 130 Park Drive, Milton Park, Abingdon, Oxon OX14 4SE. Telephone: (44) 01235 400555. Email primary@bookpoint.co.uk. Lines are open from 9 a.m. to 5 p.m., Monday to Saturday, with a 24-hour message answering service.

Parents, Tutors please call: (44) 020 3122 6405 (Monday to Friday, 9.30 a.m. to 4.30 p.m.). Email: parentenquiries@galorepark.co.uk

Visit our website at www.galorepark.co.uk for details of other revision guides for Common Entrance, examination papers and Galore Park publications.

ISBN: 978 1 4718 6717 0

Text copyright © Nigel Pearce 2018

First published in 2018 by
Galore Park Publishing Ltd,
An Hachette UK Company
Carmelite House
50 Victoria Embankment
London EC4Y 0DZ

www.galorepark.co.uk

Impression number   10 9 8 7 6 5 4 3 2 1

Year   2022 2021 2020 2019 2018

Cover photo © Getty Images/iStockphoto/Thinkstock

Illustrations by Integra Software Services

Typeset in ITC Officina Sans Std book 11.5/13 by Integra Software Services Pvt. Ltd., Pondicherry, India
Printed in Slovenia by DZS Grafik D.O.O.

A catalogue record for this title is available from the British Library.

Table des matières

Introduction

About this book

Originally entitled *So You Really Want to Learn French*, the course has been thoroughly revised under its new title *French for Common Entrance*, and much new work relevant to the latest ISEB examination syllabus has been included. Because students start French at different times, the course is written with full awareness of the two levels at which Common Entrance French may be taken. Suggestions as to how the course may be used for students approaching the exam at different levels may be found in the *Teacher Notes and Answers* (available as a PDF download).

Why French looks different

One of the first things a student will notice about French is the *accents*. They tell you how to pronounce parts of a word and can distinguish one word from another spelled the same.

1 **The acute accent** (l'accent aigu)
   Written over the letter 'e' this makes it sound like the 'é' sound in 'café', for example: bébé (baby)
2 **The grave accent** (l'accent grave)
   Written over the letter 'e', this makes it sound similar to the vowel in the English word 'bed', for example: crème (cream).
   Written over an 'a', it makes no change to the sound, but does differentiate certain words, for example: il a (he has), à (to/at).
3 **The circumflex accent** (l'accent circonflexe)
   Written over a vowel, this gives the letter 'e' the same sound as 'è', for example: fête (holiday/party).
4 **The cedilla** (la cédille)
   Written under a 'c', this softens the sound from a 'k' to an 's' sound, for example: ça (that).

Note that the acute, grave and circumflex accents are often not written over capital letters, but are included in this publication so that students learn the correct spellings.

Notes on features in this book

Exam style Exercice ──────────────────────────────────

Exam-style exercises have been included to help familiarise yourself with the format of the exam. Where these are specific to either Level 1 or 2, the following icons are used. All other exam-style exercises are relevant for both levels.

Level 1 exercises **Level 1**   Level 2 exercises **Level 2**

Exercises originally designed for specific skills are shown by symbols, although, of course, many exercises can be used in several different ways.

Listening   Reading   Speaking   Writing

Bonjour!

In this first chapter you will find out how to greet people, ask their names and ask how they are. You will also learn a little about France, the country where the French language was born. Did you know that it is also spoken in many other countries around the world?

Exercice 1.1

Listen to the conversation between two teachers and some pupils.

Bonjour!

Bonjour!

bonjour!	hello!	et vous?	what about you?
madame	madam, Mrs	ça va	I'm OK
monsieur	sir, Mr	salut!	hi!
ça va?	how are you?	et toi?	what about you?
ça va bien	I'm fine	très	very
merci	thank you		

1   With a partner, practise saying hello to each other in French.

2   Ask your partner how they are.

⭕ Tu or vous? Two ways to say 'you'

Which is the right word for 'you'? There are two answers to this question.

1 tu is used when 'you' is just one person.
vous is used when 'you' is more than one person.
2 tu is used when we are talking to a friend, a pet or a member of our family.
vous is used when we don't know the person well, for example a teacher or a shop assistant.

After words like et, tu becomes toi: Et toi?

vous never changes: Et vous?

⭕ Je m'appelle (giving or asking names)

To say our names, we use these expressions:

je m'appelle	**I** am called
tu t'appelles	**you** are called
il s'appelle	**he** is called
elle s'appelle	**she** is called

Another way of saying our name is simply to say: je suis ('I am'), for example:

Je suis Nicolas.   I am Nicolas.

When asking what someone's name is, the question Comment t'appelles-tu? can be asked in two other ways, just by changing the order of the words:

Tu t'appelles comment?

Comment tu t'appelles?

Exercice 1.2

Listen to the audio track.

2

Bonjour. Je m'appelle Monsieur Duclerc.

Bonjour, monsieur. Je m'appelle Pierre.

Bonjour, madame. Je m'appelle Robert.

Bonjour, Robert. Je m'appelle Madame Meunier.

Je m'appelle Robert. Comment t'appelles-tu?

Je suis Nicolas.

Je m'appelle Françoise. Et toi, tu t'appelles comment?

Salut, Robert. Moi, je m'appelle Claudine.

Excuse-moi. Tu t'appelles Martine?

Tu t'appelles Nicolas?

Oui, je m'appelle Nicolas.

Oui, je m'appelle Martine.

Oui, elle s'appelle Françoise.

Elle s'appelle Françoise?

je m'appelle	I am called/my name is	elle	she
comment t'appelles-tu?	what is your name?	il s'appelle	he is called
moi	me	elle s'appelle	she is called
et	and	je suis	I am
tu t'appelles	you are called	excuse-moi!	excuse me!
je	I	oui	yes
il	he	non	no

1 With a partner, practise saying what you are called to each other in French.

2 Ask your partner what he or she is called.

Exercice 1.3

3

Listen to the audio track. You should notice people asking others what their name is and how they answer. Listen a few times so you get used to these expressions.

le nouveau professeur	the new teacher	c'est ça	that's right
n'est-ce pas?	isn't that so?	au revoir	goodbye
alors	so,		

Now get into groups and practise similar conversations, saying 'hello' and introducing yourself in French. Then say goodbye.

Exercice 1.4

Comment dit-on ... en français? – **How does one say ... in French?**

Give the French for:

1 goodbye

2 he

3 she

Choose your answers from these words. One of them is not needed!

bonjour	elle	au revoir	il

Exercice 1.5

Give the French for:

1 She is called

2 He is called

3 Hello, my name is

4 What is your name?

◯ C'est bon! – It's good!

The French for 'good' is bon. You have already met this word when you learned to say 'hello': bonjour, which actually means 'good day'. Here are some other expressions using bon:

bonsoir!	good evening!	bon appétit!	enjoy your meal!
bonne nuit!	good night!	bonne chance!	good luck!
bon anniversaire!	happy birthday!	bon voyage!	have a good journey!

And then, of course, there is the French for a sweet: un bonbon!

C'est bon, n'est-ce pas? It's good, isn't it?

Exercice 1.6

Write down a conversation between two people greeting each other. Try to use as many of the new expressions you have learnt as you can.

Draw a picture with speech bubbles in French to go with it.

Practise the conversation with a partner.

Exercice 1.7

Role play

Work in pairs. Prepare and practise this conversation.

A.

What is your name?

My name is [?]

No, he is called [?]

B.

I am called [?] What about you?

[Point to another person] Is he called Charles?

Exercice 1.8

Choose the correct answer.

1 Il/Elle s'appelle … (Charles/Sophie)

2 Comment t'appelles-…? (tu/vous)

3 Je m'appelle … (imagine the je is you yourself!)

4 Et …? (toi/vous) Comment tu t'appelles?

5 Elle s'appelle … (Marie/Philippe)

Exercice 1.9

Listen to the audio track. Try to follow the audio by reading the passage at the same time.

Je m'appelle Sophie Legrand. J'habite à Saintes en France. À l'école j'ai deux amis, Jean et Robert. Robert habite à La Rochelle et Jean habite à Nantes. J'ai aussi deux amies, Marie-Claude et Chantal. Marie-Claude habite à Saintes, comme Chantal. Et toi? Où habites-tu? Tu habites en Angleterre?

j'habite	I live	à Nantes	in Nantes
à Saintes	in Saintes	il/elle habite	he/she lives
en France	in France	aussi	also
à l'école	at school	comme	like
j'ai	I have	où	where
deux amis	two friends (*m.*)	tu habites	you live
deux amies	two friends (*f.*)	en Angleterre	in England

Say which words would come in the gaps.

1 Sophie habite à … .

2 Robert … à Saintes.

3 Sophie a deux …, Robert et Jean.

4 Sophie a deux amies, … et Chantal.

5 Marie-Claude habite à … .

> Reminder: a = 'has' but à (with the accent) = 'to', 'in' or 'at' (depending on which is best in English).

Exercice 1.10

La carte de France – Map of France

Copy the map of France. Use an atlas or the internet to identify the following towns, for example: 12 Avignon

Avignon	Marseille
Bordeaux	Nantes
Brest	Nice
Calais	Orléans
La Rochelle	Paris
Le Havre	Rouen
Lyon	Toulouse

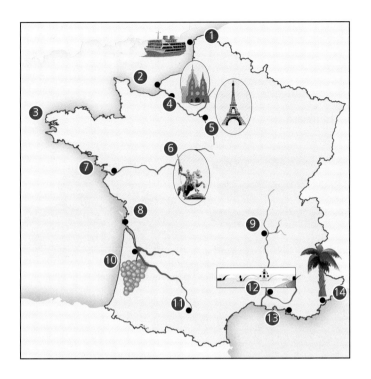

Les nombres – Numbers

Here are the numbers 1–12:

5

un(e)	one	sept	seven
deux	two	huit	eight
trois	three	neuf	nine
quatre	four	dix	ten
cinq	five	onze	eleven
six	six	douze	twelve

Reminder: The French for 'one' is also the French for 'a',
and can be either asculine (un) or feminine (une). There
is more on this in the next chapter.

Exercice 1.11

Listen to the audio while you look at the pictures.

Help Madame Martin with her weekly order from the boulangerie, as in the example:

huit croissants, s'il vous plaît   eight croissants, please.

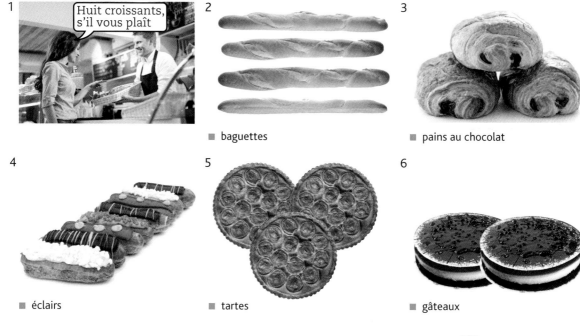

1   Huit croissants, s'il vous plaît

2   ■ baguettes

3   ■ pains au chocolat

4   ■ éclairs

5   ■ tartes

6   ■ gâteaux

Exercice 1.12

Les mathématiques

Look at the picture.

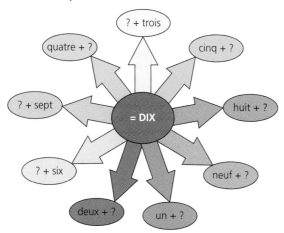

? + trois

quatre + ?

cinq + ?

? + sept

huit + ?

= DIX

? + six

neuf + ?

deux + ?

un + ?

Fill in the missing numbers so that the answer to the sums is always ten.

La salle de classe

In this chapter you will learn all about the classroom and the things we find in it. You will find out how to say where things are; you will also learn more about how the French language works.

- la télévision / la télé
- la trousse
- la gomme
- la règle
- la table
- la lampe
- l'ordinateur (m.)
- la fenêtre
- le sac
- le stylo
- le crayon
- la carte
- le tableau
- le cahier
- le livre
- la porte
- le pupitre
- la fille (une élève)
- le garçon (un élève)
- le professeur (le prof) / la professeuse (la prof)

○ Masculin ou féminin? – Masculine or feminine?

In English, whenever we use 'he' or 'she', we are generally talking about people or animals. But in French, *all* nouns are either **masculine** (male) or **feminine** (female).

You may have noticed that some of the words at the begining of this chapter have le in front of them; some have la. The French for 'the' is le if the word is **masculine**, la if it is **feminine**, for example:

le crayon   the pencil   la porte   the door

In the same way, the French for 'a' is un if the word is **masculine**, une if it is **feminine**:

un stylo   a pen   une règle   a ruler

○ Qu'est-ce que c'est? – What is it?

The best translation for 'What is this?' or 'What is it?' is Qu'est-ce que c'est?. The answer will probably begin with C'est ('It is'):

Qu'est-ce que c'est?   What is this?/What is it?
C'est une salle de classe.   It's a classroom.

○ Classroom instructions and questions

Things your teacher may say to the whole class (plural)

Asseyez-vous!	Sit down!	Fermez la fenêtre!	Close the window!
Allez, au travail!	Right, to work!	Copiez!	Copy!
Ouvrez vos livres!	Open your books!	Écoutez!	Listen!
Ouvrez vos livres à la page 10!	Open your books at page 10!	Écrivez!	Write!
Ouvrez la fenêtre!	Open the window!	Mettez-vous à deux!	Get into pairs!
		Parlez!	Speak!
		Levez-vous!	Stand up!

Things your teacher might say to individuals (singular)

Philippe, travaille avec Suzanne!   Philippe, work with Suzanne!
Georges, ferme la porte, s'il te plaît! Georges, close the door, please!

Questions teachers might ask …

On est quel jour?   What day is it?
On est le combien?   What date is it?
Où est ton cahier?   Where is your exercise book?

… and answers you might give

On est jeudi.   It is Thursday.
On est le 2 mai.   It is 2 May.
Il est dans mon sac.   It is in my bag.

There are several ways to say 'it is' – you can see two of them in the phrases above. They are explained during the course.

Listen to your teacher pronounce these expressions and try to learn them, one at a time. Test each other, with one of you playing the part of the teacher.

Exercice 2.1

Je pense à quelque chose.   I am thinking of something.

With a partner, take it in turns to think of one of the items at the beginning of this chapter. Your partner should try to guess what you are thinking of, for example:

Je pense à quelque chose.

– C'est un livre?

Non.

– C'est un crayon?

Non.

– C'est une règle?

Oui!

Exercice 2.2

Listen to the audio track.

qu'est-ce que ...?	what ...?	tu as	you have
qu'est-ce qu'il y a?	what is there?	dans	in
il y a	there is/are	ton/ta/tes	your
des	some	j'ai	I have
beaucoup de	lots of	mon/ma/mes	my
aussi	also		

1 Describe the classroom as much as you can, in English.

2 What does Françoise have in her pencil case?

3 Can you hear words in the audio that could mean 'my'? (It's all explained below.)

4 How do you say 'your pencil case'? Can you work out how you would say 'your pen' and 'your pencils'? (Again, it's all explained below.)

All the different words for 'the', 'a', 'my' and 'your'

The French words for 'the', 'a', 'my' and 'your' change their forms, depending on whether the word they are going with is masculine, feminine, singular or plural. Here is a summary.

	Singular		Plural	
	m.	*f.*	*m.*	*f.*
the	le (l')	la (l')	les	les
a/some	un	une	des	des
my	mon	ma	mes	mes
your	ton	ta	tes	tes

For example:

le crayon	la règle	les crayons	les règles
un crayon	une règle	des crayons	des règles
mon crayon	ma règle	mes crayons	mes règles

1 l' is used instead of le or la before a vowel, for example:
   l'ami   the friend
   l'élève   the pupil
2 The plural of 'a' is 'some':
   des crayons some pencils

3 The 's' at the end of French words is not usually pronounced, except as a link before a word beginning with a vowel or silent 'h':

les amis   the friends (the 's' of les is pronounced; the 's' of amis is not)

les hôtels   the hotels (the 's' of les is pronounced; the 's' of hôtels is not)

4 mon and ton are used with feminine nouns (rather than ma and ta) if these begin with a vowel or silent 'h':

mon amie   my friend (*f.*)

ton histoire   your story

Exercice 2.3

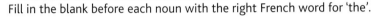

Fill in the blank before each noun with the right French word for 'the'.

1   ... livre (*m.*)

2   ... trousse (*f.*)

3   ... table (*f.*)

4   ... fenêtres (*pl.*)

5   ... école (*f.*) (notice the vowel)

6 ... sac (*m.*)

7 ... gomme (*f.*)

8 ... stylos (*pl.*)

9 ... règles (*pl.*)

10 ... ordinateur (*m.*) (notice the vowel)

Exercice 2.4

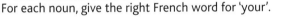

For each noun, give the right French word for 'your'.

1 ... crayon (*m.*)

2 ... ami (*m.*)

3 ... amie (*f.*) (amie is feminine, but starts with a vowel!)

4 ... cartes (*pl.*)

5 ... profs (*pl.*)

6 ... règle (*f.*)

7 ... livre (*m.*)

8 ... trousse (*f.*)

9 ... cahiers (*pl.*)

10 ... gomme (*f.*)

Exercice 2.5

Match up the English with the correct French, for example: **1 = h**.

1 **my book**	**(a)** ma carte
2 my teacher	**(b)** mon stylo
3 the doors	**(c)** ma trousse
4 my map	**(d)** les portes
5 my pencil case	**(e)** mon professeur
6 my pen	**(f)** un écran
7 a screen	**(g)** des filles
8 my class	**(h)** mon livre
9 some girls	**(i)** des garçons
10 some boys	**(j)** ma classe

Exercice 2.6

Listen to the audio track then answer the questions below the vocabulary.

regarde	look (at)	la calculatrice/la calculette	the calculator
le tableau blanc	the whiteboard	mais	but
une étagère	a shelf	c'est	it is
voici	here is	la chaise	the chair

1 What is in Pierre's classroom?

2 What is in Anne-Marie's pencil case?

3 What do we learn about Pierre's calculator?

Exercice 2.7

With a partner, make up some questions asking where things are, for example:

Où est ton stylo?

– Voici mon stylo!

⭕ De (d' before a vowel) – Of (showing possession)

In French, the only way to say (for example):

Sophie's pencil case

is to change it into

The pencil case of Sophie   La trousse de Sophie

Make up a few examples of your own. Choose an object and the person it belongs to, for example:

Le crayon de Patrick   Patrick's pencil (The pencil of Patrick)

La trousse d'Amélie   Amélie's pencil case (The pencil case of Amélie)

The French for 'of the …' is du (*m.*), de la (*f.*), de l' (before a vowel or silent 'h') or des (*pl.*), for example:

La trousse du garçon   The boy's pencil case (The pencil case of the boy)

La classe des élèves   The pupils' classroom (The classroom of the pupils)

Before la or l' we do not need to change anything, for example:

La trousse de la fille   The girl's pencil case (The pencil case of the girl)

La classe de l'élève   The pupil's classroom (The classroom of the pupil)

Exercice 2.8

Write the English equivalent of these sentences.

1 le livre de Sophie   4 l'ordinateur du professeur

2 la trousse de Paul   5 le sac de la fille

3 la calculette de Charlotte

Verbs – An introduction

Verbs are the words we use to show people 'doing', 'having', 'being', 'thinking' and so on.

A verb helps a sentence make sense; without a verb, you do not have a complete sentence.

For every **one** verb in French, there are **two** options in English*:

French	English
je chante	I sing *or* I am singing
tu chantes	you sing *or* you are singing
il chante	he sings *or* he is singing
elle chante	she sings *or* she is singing

* in the present tense

The word je ('I') becomes j' before a vowel or silent 'h'.

You will meet more **verbs** as you progress, especially in the next chapter.

For the rest of this chapter, we shall be learning how to talk about people:

having (for example 'he *has* a red pen')

and

being (for example 'he *is* French').

○ Les verbes: avoir ('to have')

The expressions we'll need for talking about *having* are:

avoir: to have			
j'ai	I have	nous avons	we have
tu as	you (*sing.*) have	vous avez	you (*pl.*) have
il a	he has	ils ont	they (*m.*) have
elle a	she has	elles ont	they (*f.*) have

Don't try to learn these all at once. As you work through the chapter, keep looking back at this page to make sure you are using the right word. Eventually you will know it thoroughly.

When we use a name, or something else like 'the boy' or 'my friend', before 'has', we use the same verb as for 'he' or 'she', just as we do in English:

il a	he has	le garçon a	the boy has
Philippe a	Philippe has	mon ami a	my friend has
Chantal a	Chantal has		

Exercice 2.9

Listen, look at the pictures and complete the sentences, as in the example:

Il a un cahier? Oui, il a un cahier.

Il a un cahier?

Oui, il ...

Elle a une gomme?

Oui, ...

Vous avez des crayons?

Oui, nous ...

Vous avez des étagères dans la classe?

Oui, ...

Ils ont un ordinateur dans la classe?

Oui, ...

Exercice 2.10

Choose the right part of avoir to fill each gap.

1 J'… un cahier.

2 Tu … un livre.

3 Il … des crayons.

4 Elles … des trousses.

5 Tu … les cahiers de Chantal?

6 Marc … les stylos de Jean.

7 Vous … une règle?

8 Elle … ta trousse.

9 Mon ami … une gomme.

10 Oui, il … des cartes.

Les verbes: être ('to be')

11

To talk about who, what or where things or people *are*, we use the verb être. Look at these expressions:

être: to be			
je suis	I am	nous sommes	we are
tu es	you (*sing*.) are	vous êtes	you (*pl*.) are
il est	he is	ils sont	they (*m*.) are
elle est	she is	elles sont	they (*f*.) are

Again, don't try to learn these all at once. As you work through the chapter, keep looking back at this page to make sure you are using the right word. Eventually you will know these thoroughly.

As before, when we use a name, or something else like 'the boy' or 'my friend', before 'is', we use the same verb as for 'he' or 'she', just as we do in English:

il est	he is	le garçon est	the boy is
Philippe est	Philippe is	mon ami est	my friend is
Chantal est	Chantal is		

La rentrée – Back to school

The start of a new school year (la rentrée) can be a confusing time, even for teachers!

Look at the conversation and see how many words from the verb être you can find:

Nicolas. Bonjour, monsieur, je suis Nicolas.

Prof. Bonjour, Nicolas. Tu es dans ma classe?

Nicolas. Oui, monsieur.

Prof.	Il est dans ma classe?
Sonia.	Oui, monsieur.
Prof.	Et vous, vous êtes aussi dans ma classe?
Georges et Marie.	Oui, monsieur, nous sommes aussi dans la classe!
Prof.	Et Sophie et Anne, elles sont dans ma classe?
Georges et Marie.	Oui, monsieur!
Prof.	Et les garçons?
Georges et Marie.	Oui!
Pierre.	Il est fou*, le prof!
* fou	mad, crazy

Exercice 2.11

Choose the right part of être to fill each gap.

1   Je ... Nicolas.

2   Il ... dans la classe.

3   Vous ... dans ma classe?

4   Nous ... dans la classe.

5   Les filles ... dans la classe.

6   Le prof ... fou!

7   Où ... ma règle?

8   Elle ... dans ta trousse!

9   Mon stylo ... dans mon sac?

10 Oui, il ... dans ton sac.

Reminder: The word for 'it' is il when referring to a masculine noun, elle when referring to a feminine one.

Exercice 2.12

12

Listen to the audio track, which is a conversation about where things are, then try answering the questions. You will hear:

où est ...?   where is ...?   où sont ...?   where are ...?

and lots of words helping us say where things are:

rouge	red	où est/sont?	where is/are?
le ballon	the ball	devant	in front of
le dictionnaire	the dictionary	derrière	behind
la radio	the radio	sous	under
le placard	the cupboard	sur	on top of, on
les devoirs	the homework	à côté de	next to
zut!	bother!	entre	between
la poubelle	the bin		

1 Here are the questions. Answer them in English.

  (a) Where is Charles's geography book?

  (b) What is next to Catherine's red pen?

  (c) Where is Charles's bag?

  (d) What is behind his bag?

  (e) What has Charles put in the bin?

2 Look at the picture. With a partner, make up some questions and answers, as in the examples:

Où est la trousse?

– Elle est sur le pupitre.

Où est le sac?

– Il est sous la table.

Exercice 2.13

13

Prof.   Bonjour, Marc. Tu as ta trousse?

Marc.   Bonjour, monsieur. Oui, j'ai ma trousse ici. J'ai aussi mon livre de français et mon cahier de maths.

Prof.   Qu'est-ce que tu as dans ta trousse?

Marc.   J'ai cinq crayons et deux stylos, ma règle, ma calculatrice et une gomme.

Prof.   Tu as deux stylos?

Marc.   Oui. J'ai mon stylo et le stylo de Pierre.

Prof.   Ah. Le stylo de Pierre est rouge?

Marc.   Oui, monsieur, il est rouge.

1 Listen to the audio track as you read, then do the exercises.

Look at the conversation again. Choose the right word from the box below for each gap.

As always, check earlier in the chapter to make sure you are right.

(a) Marc ... deux stylos.

(b) Le ... dit*: «Bonjour, Marc.»

(c) Marc répond**: «... , monsieur.»

(d) ... stylo de Pierre ... rouge.

(e) Marc dit*: «J'ai cinq ... ... deux ....»

a	bonjour	crayons	est
prof	et	stylos	Le

* dit   (he/she) says   ** répond   (he/she) answers

2 Are these sentences true (vrai) or false (faux)?

(a) Le garçon s'appelle Philippe.

(b) Le professeur s'appelle Monsieur Laclos.

(c) Il y a deux stylos dans la trousse de Marc.

(d) Le stylo de Marc est rouge.

(e) Marc a trois livres.

3 Match up the sentence halves below so they make sense. Simply write a letter for each number.

Example: (a) (v): Le stylo de Pierre est rouge.   Pierre's pen is red.

(a) Le stylo de Pierre est

(b) Marc a deux

(c) Le garçon

(d) Marc a un

(e) Il répond:

(i) livre de français.

(ii) s'appelle Marc.

(iii) «Bonjour, monsieur.»

(iv) stylos dans sa trousse.

(v) rouge.

Exercice 2.14

Give the right French word(s) for each of the English words in brackets.

1 Marc (is) dans la salle de classe (of) Pierre.

2 Il (has) ma trousse. Dans la trousse (there are) mes crayons.

3 La règle de Sophie est (in) la trousse (of) Anne-Marie.

4 (The) calculatrice de Bernard (is) rouge.

5 Le (boy) dans la salle de classe (is called) Pierre.

Exercice 2.15

You will hear a short paragraph. Five classroom items are mentioned. Choose the correct ones from the list below.

14

pencil	pen	exercise book	textbook
eraser	computer	ruler	calculator

Quel âge as-tu? – How old are you?

When we say how old we are, we use avoir ('to have') rather than être ('to be'), for example:

Quel âge as-tu?	How old are you? (literally: 'What age *have* you?')
J'ai onze ans.	I am eleven. (literally: 'I *have* eleven years.')
Et le bébé?	And the baby?
Il a un an.	He is one year old (literally: 'He *has* one year.')

Exercice 2.16

Quel âge as-tu?

Give an answer for each picture.

Exercice 2.17

Using the charts 'Avoir (the verb 'to have')' and 'Être (the verb 'to be')' to help you, complete these expressions; for example for question 1, we need to say 'I have a pencil case', so we have to choose the part of avoir that goes with je (or j').

1 J'… une trousse. (avoir)

2 Tu … un cahier, Tiffany? (avoir)

3 Monsieur Béchet … devant la classe. (être)

4 Tu … un stylo? (avoir)

5 Je … Nicolas (être) et j'… onze ans. (avoir)

If you have time, try these extra ones:

6 J'… trois crayons.

7 Alors Charles et moi, nous … douze ans.

8 Les élèves dans la salle de classe … des livres.

9 Philippe … un ami de Charles.

10 Nicolas … une amie qui s'appelle Chantal.

Exercice 2.18

Try to unscramble these words! They are all items or people you will find in the classroom. If you find it difficult, ask your teacher to give you some hints.

1	SLOTY	5	ÇROGNA
2	MOGEM	6	LELFI
3	AERTC	7	EUROSPREFS
4	EORPT	8	CLARELACCITU

Dans ma salle de classe – In my classroom

A memory game

Take it in turns to think of an item that you might have in your classroom. The list should get longer and longer, as in this example:

Dans ma salle de classe, il y a un stylo.

Dans ma salle de classe, il y a un stylo et des crayons.

Dans ma salle de classe, il y a un stylo, des crayons et un ordinateur.

The winner is the one who can make the longest list without mistakes.

Chez nous

In this chapter you will learn how to describe your home, and about a typical French breakfast.

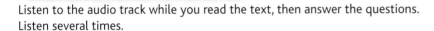

Listen to the audio track while you read the text, then answer the questions. Listen several times.

Voici Georges

■ Georges est dans la salle de bains

Voici Martine

■ Martine est dans sa chambre

Georges.	Mmm, le petit déjeuner!
Maman.	Georges! Tu es dans la salle de bains?
Georges.	Non, maman. J'arrive.
Maman.	Martine! Tu es dans ta chambre?
Martine.	Non, maman, j'arrive tout de suite! Tu manges déjà, papa?
Papa.	Oui, Martine. Je mange mon petit-déjeuner.
Martine.	J'adore le petit déjeuner!
Papa.	Il est bon, le café.

Georges et Martine sont dans la cuisine. Maman prépare le petit-déjeuner. Papa regarde le journal. Georges mange une tartine avec son thé et Martine mange un croissant avec son chocolat. Ils mangent le petit-déjeuner. Martine aime les croissants; ils sont délicieux! Georges adore les tartines; elles sont délicieuses!

la salle de bains	the bathroom	le thé	the tea
la chambre	the bedroom	le chocolat	hot chocolate, chocolate
la cuisine	the kitchen	le croissant	the croissant
le journal	the newspaper	le café	the coffee
regarder	to look at	délicieux	delicious
préparer	to prepare	aimer	to like
j'arrive	I'm coming	adorer	to love
tout de suite	right away	le petit-déjeuner	the breakfast
déjà	already	une tartine	a tartine*
manger	to eat	avec	with

*A tartine is a slice of bread with butter and jam or chocolate spread, for example.

Checking the text above, give the correct versions of these sentences in English:

1 Georges loves croissants.

2 Martine is eating a tartine.

3 Martine loves tartines.

4 Papa makes breakfast.

5 Maman looks at the newspaper.

◯ Les verbes du premier groupe – First-group verbs (-ER)

So far, you have met two rather odd-looking verbs, avoir and être. We looked at these first because they are so useful.

Now we are going to see how ordinary verbs work. In the story we have just read and listened to, we met the following verbs.

adore	(Georges adore)	Georges loves
mange	(Papa mange)	Papa eats
prépare	(Maman prépare)	Maman prepares
regarde	(Papa regarde)	Papa looks at
aime	(Martine aime)	Martine likes

We can see that these are all *doing* words.

Notice also that they all have the same ending: -e. This is because they all follow the same pattern, just as we say he **likes** and she **eats**, both with **-s** at the end in English.

Verbs in French can be put into groups, according to the pattern they follow. We call the largest group the 'first' group because it has the most verbs in it.

We also call these verbs -ER verbs, because their *infinitives* (their titles or 'names') end in -ER.

We can set these out as follows, using as our example the verb regarder:

regarder: to watch/look at	
je regarde	I watch *or* I am watching
tu regardes	you watch *or* you are watching
il regarde	he watches *or* he is watching
elle regarde	she watches *or* she is watching
nous regardons	we watch *or* we are watching
vous regardez	you watch *or* you are watching
ils regardent	they (*m.*) watch *or* they are watching
elles regardent	they (*f.*) watch *or* they are watching

You only need to learn **one** set of endings to be able to use **all** first-group verbs.

To use an -ER verb, you simply take off the -er from the title word, or *infinitive*, leaving the *stem*, and add the correct *ending* (shown in bold in the table above).

Note that je becomes j' in front of a vowel or silent 'h', for example:

j'écoute, j'habite and so on.

Exercice 3.2

Choose **one** of these verbs, then try writing out its first four parts (je, tu, il, elle).

1	arriver	to arrive	6	aimer	to like
2	chanter	to sing	7	parler	to speak
3	jouer	to play	8	écouter	to listen (to)
4	habiter	to live	9	manger	to eat
5	donner	to give			

If you finish quickly, do the plural parts, then choose another verb to practise on!

Learn the meanings of all the verbs above.

Exercice 3.3

Complete these verbs by adding the correct endings, then give *both* versions of the English for each one, for example:

je parl... – je parle   **I speak *or* I am speaking**

1 Elle jou...

2 Nous chant...

3 Je donn...

4 Marie arriv...

5 J'écout...

Exercice 3.4

Write these expressions in French. Take time to make sure you have put the right endings on.

1 I like

2 You (*sing.*) are eating

3 He is singing

4 She is eating

5 We arrive

6 You (*pl.*) love

7 They (*m.*) live

8 They (*f.*) are watching

9 We give

10 She lives

Exercice 3.5

Look at the pictures. The teacher is asking questions. Try to complete the answers with the right verb (and the right ending!), for example:

Vous chantez? Non, nous écoutons de la musique.

Exercice 3.6

Pick out the ten first-group (-ER) verbs. Make a list of them.

chiendonnerthécaféchocolatmanger

chatmaisonchantergarderclasseaimer

cahiertroussecartableêtrelaverpasser

tartinetartineradorertélévisionécouterradio

À – To/at (in)

The French for both 'to' and 'at' is à (with an accent), for example:

Elle donne une tartine à Robert.   She gives a slice of bread **to** Robert.

With some verbs, à is not necessary. Look at these examples:

Tu écoutes la radio?   Are you **listening to** the radio?

Nous regardons la voiture.   We are **looking at** the car.

Vous regardez la télé.   You are **watching** television.

Exercice 3.7

17

First, read the vocabulary below. Listen to the audio and try to answer the questions.

souvent	often	chéri (*m.*), chérie (*f.*)	my dear
une assiette	a plate	la cuiller/cuillère	the spoon
pendant que	while	le bol	the bowl
le couteau	the knife	le beurre	the butter
il/elle dit	he/she says	la cafetière	the coffee pot
encore	more	la confiture	the jam
le verre	the glass	le jus d'orange	the orange juice
		le nom	the name

1 Who is singing while she is listening to the radio?

2 What are Martine and Georges doing?

3 What does papa think of the coffee today?

4 Give two or three of the items on the table, apart from the coffee pot.

5 What is on Martine's bowl?

Choose your own French breakfast! Two items, with a choice of drink, are acceptable.

Chaz Nicolao

le petit-déjeuner

************ *8€* ************

Jus d'orange	Croissant	Pain
Chocolat	avec du beurre	au chocolat
Thé	et de la	Pain
Café	confiture	aux raisins

Aimer et adorer – Liking and loving

Notice how we use an *infinitive* after verbs such as aimer and adorer, for example:

Maman adore chanter.   Maman loves to sing. (Maman loves singing.)

■ Nicolas adore regarder la télé.   ■ Martine aime chanter. ■ Nicolas et Robert adorent manger!

What do *you* like to do?

Try to make up a few sentences like the one above.

Exercice 3.9

Role play

Imagine that you are person A in the exercise below. Follow the instructions and see if you can put together the French you need. Person B just has to say what is printed. Then change parts so your partner has a go.

A.

Hello, [?]. What is in your classroom?

What do you have in your pencil case?

It is in my bag.

Yes, there is a computer in my classroom.

B.

Bonjour. Il y a une table et dix chaises.

J'ai une gomme, un crayon et une règle. Où est ton cahier de maths?

Il y a un ordinateur dans ta classe?

Mon, ton, son – My, your, his/her

The words for 'his/her' follow the same pattern as those for 'my' and 'your'.

Here they all are together:

Masculine	Feminine	Plural	
mon	ma	mes	my
ton	ta	tes	your
son	sa	ses	his/her/its/one's

All these words have to be the same gender as the nouns they are describing. So, if I want to say 'my' house, I have to know that the word for house is **feminine.** Then I can say ma maison and it will be correct, for example:

J'aime ta maison, Nicolas.   I like **your** house, Nicolas.

Martine cherche son stylo.   Martine is looking for **her** pen. (son because stylo is masculine)

If a feminine noun begins with a vowel, the masculine form (mon, ton, son) is used, for example:

Mon école.   My school (feminine)

Son amie.   His/Her girlfriend

Finally, remember that son, sa and ses **all** mean his or her, for example:

Nicolas aime son professeur.   Nicolas likes **his** teacher.

Marie aime son professeur.   Marie likes **her** teacher.

Voici et voilà – Here is and there is

Voici mon chien.

Voilà mon chat.

Voici and voilà are used when showing something to someone or when pointing something out: voici means 'here is' and voilà 'there is'. If, however, you want to say, 'There is a dog in the house', you are just giving information, so you use il y a, for example:

Il y a un chien dans la maison.

Exercice 3.10

Say whether you would use voici, voilà or il y a for these expressions.

1 Here is her house.

2 There is his house.

3 Here is your house.

4 There is a book in her bag.

5 There is a dog in his house.

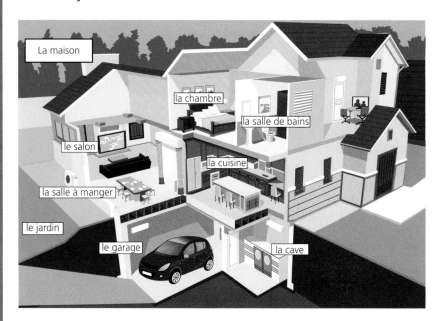

La maison

la chambre

la salle de bains

le salon

la cuisine

la salle à manger

le jardin

le garage

la cave

Voici ma maison! – Here is my house!

French homes are similar to British ones, except for a few details:

- The windows are usually protected by shutters (les volets).
- The windows open *inwards*.
- Very often the ground floor is above a cellar (which, in a modern house, includes a garage).
- Most of the floors are boarded or tiled, rather than carpeted.

Exercice 3.11

Read the vocabulary. The audio track will be played several times so you can complete the questions below.

visiter	to visit, look around	la chambre	the bedroom
à gauche	to the left	la pièce	the room
l'entrée (*f.*)	the hall	le salon	the sitting room
au rez-de-chaussée	on the ground floor	la salle à manger	the dining room
à droite	to the right	monter	to go up
à l'étage	upstairs	la salle de bains	the bathroom

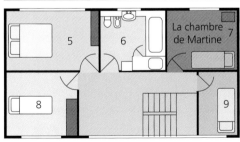

1 Match the following rooms to the numbers on the plan, for example:

    4   l'entrée

    You will need to use one word more than once.

l'entrée	le salon	la salle de bains	la salle à manger
la chambre des parents	la cuisine	la chambre de Martine	chambre

2 Draw a plan of your own home, but label the rooms in French. If you prefer, draw one for your 'ideal' home.

Level 1

Match up the sentence halves, so each long sentence makes sense.

1 Martine arrive et
2 Dans la maison,
3 Voici une photo
4 Le cahier de Sophie
5 Il y a trois livres

(a) il y a un chien et un chat.
(b) de mes parents.
(c) et douze crayons sur ma table.
(d) mange le petit-déjeuner.
(e) est sur la table.

Exercice 3.13

The verbs in these sentences are wrong. **Correct** each one for the sentence it is in.

If you have time, say also what each sentence means in English.

1 Paul mangent le petit-déjeuner. ✗
2 Maman et Charles arrivez dans la salle à manger. ✗
3 Sophie sont dans la salle de bains. ✗
4 Paul et Georges regarde la télévision. ✗
5 Marie-Claire, tu écoute la radio? ✗

◯ N'est-ce pas? – Isn't that so?

The phrase n'est-ce pas?, which we met briefly in Chapter 1, means something like 'isn't that so?' or 'don't you agree?'

Elle est anglaise, n'est-ce pas?   She is English, **isn't she**?

La vie quotidienne et l'heure

In this chapter you will learn how to tell the time in French and how to say when you do certain things every day.

La vie quotidienne – Daily life

Listen to Georges and Martine again as they get up in the morning:

■ Georges se réveille à sept heures.

■ Martine se lève à sept heures et quart.

■ Martine s'habille à sept heures vingt.

■ Georges se lave à sept heures et demie.

■ Martine et Georges descendent à huit heures moins le quart.

■ Il est huit heures. C'est l'heure du petit-déjeuner.

Let's look again at some of the photo captions:

Georges se réveille	Georges wakes up	George se lave	Georges has a wash
Martine se lève	Martine gets up	Martine s'habille	Martine gets dressed

Les verbes pronominaux – Reflexive verbs

20

Did you notice? All the French verbs in the expressions above start with se or s', because they are things you do *to yourself* – the verb equivalent of 'selfies'! We call them **reflexive** verbs.

il se réveille = he wakes (himself) up	*from*	se réveiller	to wake (oneself) up
elle se lève = she gets (herself) up	*from*	se lever	to get (oneself) up
il se lave = he washes (himself)	*from*	se laver	to wash (oneself)
elle s'habille = she dresses (herself)	*from*	s'habiller	to get (oneself) dressed

Here is the verb se laver, set out in full; the 'self' parts are shown in **bold**:

se laver: to wash oneself			
je **me** lave	I wash	nous **nous** lavons	we wash
tu **te** laves	you wash	vous **vous** lavez	you (*pl.*) wash
il **se** lave	he washes	ils **se** lavent	they (*m.*) wash
elle **se** lave	she washes	elles **se** lavent	they (*f.*) wash

> Reminder: As with any verb, expressions like je me lave can also mean 'I am washing'; elle s'habille can mean 'she is getting dressed', on so on.

Exercice 4.1

Complete the sentences with the correct reflexive verb form.

1 Elle … (se lève/me lève/te lève) dans sa chambre.

2 Je … (me lave/te lave/se lave) dans la salle de bains.

3 Vous … (me réveille/nous lavons/vous réveillez) à 7 h 25.

4 Nous … (m'habille/vous habillez/nous habillons) avant le petit-déjeuner.

5 Tu … (se réveille/me réveille/te réveilles).

Exercice 4.2

Give the French for:

1 She wakes up.

2 You (*sing.*) get dressed.

3 I wash myself.

4 You (*sing.*) wash yourself.

5 He wakes up.

Notice that me becomes m', te becomes t' and se becomes s' when these come before a vowel or a silent 'h', for example:

je m'habille, tu t'habilles, il s'habille

We often use the expressions above with a **time** expression, to say *when* we get up or *when* we go to bed, for example. So it makes sense to learn how to tell the time in French.

Quelle heure est-il? – What time is it?

Listen to the audio.

The basic formula is: il est … heures.

This tells us that it is … o'clock, for example:

il est trois heures

it is three o'clock

Other times are:

midi	12 noon
minuit	12 midnight
… heures et demie	half **past**, for example il est dix heures et demie (10.30)
… heures et quart	quarter **past**, for example il est deux heures et quart (2.15)
… heures moins le quart	quarter **to**, for example il est quatre heures moins le quart (3.45)

Notice that quatre heures moins le quart really means 'four hours **minus** the quarter', so, when it is written in figures, it will be 3 h 45.

■ Il est sept heures.

■ Il est neuf heures et quart.

■ Il est onze heures et demie.

■ Il est midi.

■ Il est cinq heures moins le quart.

■ Il est minuit.

Give me more time!

To make times clearer, or more exact, we can say du matin (in the morning), de l'après-midi (in the afternoon) or du soir (in the evening), for example:

il est trois heures de l'après-midi   it is three o'clock in the afternoon or 3 p.m.

Now we need to learn some more numbers:

Two numbers you'll need quite often are quinze (fifteen) and trente (thirty), the numbers of minutes in a quarter-hour or half-hour.

You have already learned the numbers 1 to 12 and you'll be revising numbers in Chapter 6. Meanwhile, here are some new ones:

treize	thirteen	dix-neuf	nineteen
quatorze	fourteen	vingt	twenty
quinze	fifteen	vingt et un	twenty-one
seize	sixteen	vingt-deux	twenty-two
dix-sept	seventeen	vingt-trois …	twenty-three …
dix-huit	eighteen		

and so on, until we reach:

trente	thirty

Below, you can see the difference between the way that afternoon times are shown in English-speaking countries and French.

13 h	treize heures	1 p.m.
14 h	quatorze heures	2 p.m.
15 h	quinze heures	3 p.m.
16 h	seize heures	4 p.m.
17 h	dix-sept heures	5 p.m.
18 h	dix-huit heures	6 p.m.
19 h	dix-neuf heures	7 p.m.
20 h	vingt heures	8 p.m.
21 h	vingt et une heures	9 p.m.
22 h	vingt-deux heures	10 p.m.
23 h	vingt-trois heures	11 p.m.

Exercice 4.3

1 Say these times in French, for example:

7.30 a.m. – sept heures et demie

(a) 8.00 a.m.

(b) 4.30 a.m.

(c) 3.15 a.m.

(d) 9.30 a.m.

(e) 12.00 noon

(f) 12.00 midnight

(g) 7.15 a.m.

(h) 5.45 a.m.

2 These times appear as they would in France. How would they be given in England? For example:

21 h – 9 p.m.

(a) 22 h

(b) 15 h

(c) 10 h 30

(d) 14 h 10

(e) 18 h 15

(f) 07 h 20

(g) 05 h 15

(h) 19 h 25

3 Look at these clocks and ask your partner: Quelle heure est-il?

a
b
c

d
e
f

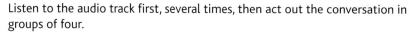

Exercice 4.4

22

Listen to the audio track first, several times, then act out the conversation in groups of four.

Martine.	Salut, papa!
Papa.	Bonjour, Martine! Bonjour, Georges!
Georges.	Bonjour, papa! Bonjour, maman! Ça va?
Maman.	Ça va, chéri. Quelle heure est-il, s'il te plaît?
Georges.	Je ne sais pas*.
Maman.	Martine, il est quelle heure?
Martine.	Il est … huit heures cinq.
Papa.	Huit heures cinq? Alors**, au revoir!
Maman.	Tu ne manges pas ta tartine?
Papa.	Ah non! Je suis en retard***!
* je ne sais pas	I don't know
** alors	so; well then
*** en retard	late

Vive la différence!

Lunch (le déjeuner) is considered by many French people to be the most important meal of the day. Shops often still close from noon until 14 h (2.00 p.m.) and schools have a longer lunch break than they do in the UK. Students may eat in the school canteen but often they go home for lunch.

Asking what time something happens

In French, we have to ask *at* what time something happens.

> Reminder: The French for 'at' is à, for example:
>
> Tu arrives à quelle heure?   (At) what time do you arrive?

Exam style | Exercice 4.5

Level 2

Role play
Take it in turns to be A and B. A follows the instructions, B reads out what is printed.

A.
What time do you get up?
What do you have for
  breakfast?
What time do you arrive at
  school?
What time do you have lunch
  at school?
I eat at home at [?] o'clock.

B.
Je me lève à sept heures.
Je mange une tartine avec du
  chocolat chaud.
D'habitute*, vers huit heures et
  quart.
À midi trente. Et toi, tu manges à
  quelle heure?

* d'habitude   usually

Les verbes: faire

23

Faire is an important French verb, because you can use it in so many different ways. It can mean 'to do' or 'to make': learn it by heart.

faire: to do/to make	
je fais	nous faisons
tu fais	vous faites
il fait	ils font
elle fait	elles font

Nicolas fait son lit.   Nicolas makes his bed.

The verb faire is used for *doing* a range of activities:

faire la cuisine to do the cooking
faire la vaisselle to do the washing-up
faire la lessive to do the (clothes) washing

faire le ménage to do the housework
faire ses devoirs to do one's homework

It is also used for some expressions in English where 'to go' is used:

faire du ski	to go skiing	faire des courses	to go shopping
faire du cheval	to go horse-riding	faire une promenade	to go for a walk

Exam style **Exercice 4.6**

24

Read the vocabulary below, listen as the audio track is played several times, then answer the questions.

aider	to help	ben …	um/well …
ranger	to tidy	sortir les poubelles	to put the bins out
faire son lit	to make one's bed	quelquefois	sometimes
tous les jours	every day		

1 What does Jacques do at home to help his parents?

2 How often does he make his bed?

3 What does Jacques do *sometimes*?

4 What does he do on Tuesdays?

Exercice 4.7

Look at the information in sentences (a) to (e) below, then say in English what happens …

1 after breakfast

2 every day

3 at seven p.m.

4 in the Alps

5 after lunch

  (a) Je fais mes devoirs à sept heures du soir.

  (b) Nous faisons des courses tous les jours.

  (c) Papa fait la vaisselle après le petit-déjeuner.

  (d) Vous faites du ski dans les Alpes.

  (e) Ils font une promenade après le déjeuner.

Exercice 4.8

Choose the right part of faire to fill the gaps.

1 Philippe … du cheval dans la forêt.

2 Moi, je … du ski à Val d'Isère.

3 Papa et Georges … la cuisine – quelquefois!

4 Elle … ses devoirs à cinq heures.

5 Nous … des courses aujourd'hui*.

* aujourd'hui   today

Exercice 4.9

Write these sentences in French.

1 He makes his bed at 7.30.

2 He does the housework at 11.00 a.m.

3 She does the washing every day.

4 They (*m.*) do the washing-up at 2.30 p.m.

5 You (*sing.*) are doing the cooking today.

Les verbes: mettre

The verb mettre means 'to put' or 'to put on' (clothing).

25

mettre: to put	
je mets	nous mett**ons**
tu mets	vous mett**ez**
il met	ils mett**ent**
elle met	elles mett**ent**

Exam style   Exercice 4.10

Checking carefully as you go, choose the right part of mettre for each gap. In the first five sentences, you are given a choice.

1 Nous … les crayons de Pierre dans sa trousse. (mettons, mettez, mettent)

2 Je …. mon pullover. (met, mets, mettent)

3 Ils … les cahiers sur la table. (mettent, mettez, mettons)

4 Maman … la table pour le petit-déjeuner. (mettons, mets, met)

5 Vous … le café dans le bol. (mets, met, mettez)

6 Il … mon sac dans la salle de classe.

7 Elle … un poster dans ta chambre?

8 Tu … la table?

Exercice 4.11

Say what you do to help at home.

Use some or all of the expressions in the list below.

Don't forget to use the right part of the verb for je:

je sors …   je promène …   je mets …   je débarrasse …

je range …   je donne …   je passe…   je fais …

sortir les poubelles	to put the bins out	faire la vaisselle	to do the washing-up
ranger ma chambre	to tidy my room	faire le tri	to sort the rubbish
donner à manger au chat	to feed the cat	quelquefois	sometimes
promener le chien	to walk the dog	toujours	always
passer l'aspirateur	to vacuum	tous les jours	every day
mettre la table	to lay the table	d'habitude	usually
faire la cuisine	to do the cooking	souvent	often
débarrasser la table	to clear the table	rarement	rarely

Qui fait la cuisine chez toi?

D'habitude c'est maman…

■ …mais quelquefois c'est papa.

■ Ma sœur sort quelquefois les poubelles …

■ … mais elle ne promène pas le chien.

La négation – The negative (saying 'not')

To make a sentence negative ('not'), we put **ne** in front of the verb and **pas** after it.

In English, this is when we say something does **not** happen or is **not** true. Note than ne becomes n' before a vowel or silent 'h'.

Marie-Yvonne mange beaucoup.	Marie-Yvonne eats a lot.
Marie-Yvonne **ne** mange **pas** beaucoup.	Marie-Yvonne does not eat a lot.

Affirmatif		Négatif	
Elle nage	She swims	Elle **ne** nage **pas**	She does **not** swim
Ils écoutent	They listen	Ils **n'**écoutent **pas**	They do **not** listen
Il mange	He eats	Il **ne** mange **pas**	He does **not** eat
Il écoute	He is listening	Il **n'**écoute **pas**	He is **not** listening
Ils nagent	They are swimming	Ils **ne** nagent **pas**	They are **not** swimming

Exam style — Exercice 4.12

Vrai ou faux?

Listen to the audio track then decide if the statements below are true or false – vrai ou faux.

Reminder: si! means 'yes!' (in disagreement or contradiction).

ça dépend	it depends	après	after
avant	before	fatigué(e)	tired
le soir	(in) the evening		

1 Cédric *(the second speaker)* watches television after dinner.

2 Cédric does his homework after dinner.

3 Patrick does the same as Cédric.

4 Patrick watches television instead.

5 Patrick does not work in the evening as he is tired.

Exercice 4.13

Identify the verbs in these sentences, then make them negative, for example:

Marie fait son lit.   **Verb:** fait   **Negative:** ne fait pas

1 Patrick fait ses devoirs.   4 Je sors les poubelles.

2 Mélanie passe l'aspirateur.   5 Maman met toujours la table.

3 Linda fait la vaisselle.

Exam style Exercice 4.14

Level 2

Translate these sentences into French, using the words below each sentence to help you.

1 Usually, I don't do my homework at school.

d'habitude, faire, devoirs (*m.pl.*), école (*f.*)

2 My father does not watch TV in the evening.

père (*m.*), regarder, télévision (*f.*), soir (*m.*)

3 Claude and Françoise do not come downstairs before 10.00 a.m.

descendre, avant, heures (*f.pl.*)

4 Paul, you don't like your coffee?

aimer, café (*m.*)

5 I do not listen to the radio.

écouter, radio (*f.*)

On va à l'école!

In this chapter we will look at a typical school day, the school itself and how to give opinions about some subjects.

Tu vas à l'école en voiture?

Non, je vais à l'école en train. J'habite loin.

Reminder: loin = far away

Les verbes: aller

28

Un verbe très important! – A very important verb!

In order to say how we get from A to B, we need to use the verb aller ('to go'). It is therefore very important to learn it well as soon as possible.

aller: to go	
je vais	nous allons
tu vas	vous allez
il va	ils vont
elle va	elles vont

Reminder: Remember the *two* meanings in English of each of these single expressions.

You will see why this is particularly important with aller later in the course.

je vais   I go *or* I am going

tu vas   you go *or* you are going

il va   he goes *or* he is going

elle va   she goes *or* she is going ...

... and so on.

Les transports – Transport

Look at the pictures.

- en voiture

- à vélo

- en taxi

- en train

- en bateau

- à pied

- en avion

- à moto / en moto

- en car

Exercice 5.1

1 Fill in the gaps with the right part of aller and the right method of transport, for example:

Nicolas va à l'école en taxi.

(a) Marc … à l'école …

(d) Je … chez moi …

(b) Nous … à Paris …

(e) Ils … à Calais …

(c) Tu … à Nice …

(f) Vous … à l'école …

Here are a few other ways to travel that you might enjoy:

en vélomoteur (*m.*)	by moped	en métro (*m.*)	by underground ('Tube')
en scooter (*m.*)	by scooter	en tramway (*m.*)	by tram
en hélicoptère (*m.*)	by helicopter		

and some signs that you may recognise:

Accueil	Reception	Départ	Departure
Aéroport	Airport	Embarquement	Boarding
Arrivée	Arrival	Enregistrement	Check-in
Car-ferry	Car ferry	Renseignements	Information
Débarquement	Unloading	Tunnel sous la Manche	Channel Tunnel

2 Et toi, comment aimes-tu voyager?

(a) Say how you like to travel, by using the phrase j'aime voyager … and any of the ways listed above.

(b) Make up a conversation with a partner and perform it in front of the class.

Exercice 5.2

Role play

Work in pairs. Take turns to be A and B: A follows the instructions, while B reads out what is printed.

> Reminder: how …?   comment …?

A.

Hello. How do you like travel?
No, I prefer to go by train.
I prefer the train because it is
    fast and comfortable.
Yes, when* I'm not in town.
[?]
Do you go to school by bus?

B.

J'aime aller en voiture. Et toi?
Pourquoi?
Tu aimes faire du vélo?

Tu habites loin**?
Moi, j'habite ici en ville.
Oui, c'est facile.

* when   quand

** loin   far, a long way away

Les jours de la semaine – Days of the week

The days of the week in French are all masculine nouns. Note that they do not begin with a capital letter (unless they happen to be the first word in a sentence).

lundi	Monday	vendredi	Friday
mardi	Tuesday	samedi	Saturday
mercredi	Wednesday	dimanche	Sunday
jeudi	Thursday		

If we want to say 'Mondays', we use les and the day of the week in the plural, for example:

J'aime les lundis.   I like Mondays.

To say 'on Monday', we do not need a word for 'on'; we simply say lundi, for example:

Je vais à l'école lundi.   I am going to school on Monday.

If we want to say 'on Mondays', we use le and keep the day of the week singular, for example:

Je vais à l'école le lundi.   I go to school on Mondays.

Finally, if we want to say 'every Monday', we use tous les and the day of the week in the plural, for example:

Je vais à l'école tous les lundis.   I go to school every Monday.

Les matières scolaires – School subjects

School subjects (les matières, *f.pl.*) are normally easy to recognise, but here are the most common ones for you to learn:

les arts plastiques	art	les sports	sports
le dessin	drawing	les SVT (sciences de la vie et de la terre)	Earth/life sciences
les langues	languages		
le latin	Latin	les travaux manuels	craft
l'allemand	German	la technologie	technology
l'anglais	English	l'EPS (Éducation physique et sportive)	PE
le français	French		
l'espagnol	Spanish	l'instruction civique	PSE
les sciences	science	l'instruction religieuse*	RE
la biologie	biology		
la chimie	chemistry	la musique	music
la physique	physics	l'informatique	IT
les maths	maths	l'histoire-géo**	history and geography

* except in private denominational schools, religion is not taught at school in France

** a combined subject in French schools

Read the vocabulary below. Listen several times to the audio and complete the exercises.

discuter	to chat	la pause	(the) break
préféré(e)	favourite	beaucoup	very much; many
pourquoi?	why?	parler	to speak
parce que/ parce qu'	because	travailler	to work
		détester	to hate

1 Give a word for each gap:

   (a) C'est ... matin. (mercredi/jeudi/mardi)

   (b) Marie-Claire et Paul vont à l'école ... (à vélo/en bus/à pied)

   (c) La matière préférée de Marie-Claire, c'est ... (les sciences/les maths/ le latin)

   (d) Paul ... le mardi à l'école. (aime/n'aime pas/adore)

   (e) La matière préférée de Paul, c'est ... (les sciences /l'histoire-géo/les maths)

2 Write the correct ending for each verb, for example: **nous arriv ... = nous arriv<u>ons</u>**.

   (a) Paul et sa sœur Marie-Claire aim... le collège.

   (b) Paul détest... l'allemand.

   (c) Les amis discut... dans la cour pendant* la pause.

   (d) Nous parl... beaucoup avant les classes.

   (e) J'ador... le lundi.

   * pendant = during

3 Write out your school timetable in French. Use your artistic skill to make going to school really attractive! Remember: *no* English!

4 Write an email to a friend about your school. Write between 80 and 120 words. You must mention at least **four** of the points below:

● Ta salle de classe	Your classroom
● Comment tu vas à l'école	How you get to school
● Les jours que tu aimes à l'école et pourquoi	What days you like at school and why
● Les jours que tu n'aimes pas à l'école et pourquoi	The days you dislike at school and why
● À quelle heure tu vas à l'école et rentres à la maison	What time you go to school and go home

5 On va à l'école!

Exercice 5.4

Listen to the audio track, then fill in the gaps with the correct answers.

31

1 The time is ... (8 h 20/18 h 20/10 h 20).

2 Paul has ... (German/Spanish/English) in ten minutes.

3 Today, it is ... (Wednesday/Tuesday/Monday).

4 Marie-Claire does not like ... (chemistry/history/biology).

○ Les adjectifs – Adjectives (words used for describing)

Adjectives are words that describe nouns. In French, an adjective must *agree* with the noun that it describes.

This means that, if the noun is masculine, the adjective must be masculine. If the noun is feminine, the adjective must be feminine. If the noun is plural, the adjective must be plural.

In dictionaries and textbooks, adjectives are always listed in their masculine singular forms. To make an adjective feminine, we generally add an e – unless it already ends in e, in which case we leave it alone:

intelligent(e)	This shows that the feminine form of intelligent is intelligente.
fatigué(e)	This shows that the feminine form of fatigué is fatiguée.
sévère	This shows that the feminine form of sévère is the same as the masculine.

Paul est intelligent. Anne est intelligente.

Making adjectives *plural* is explained in Chapter 7.

Exercice 5.5

Listen to the adjectives pronounced on the audio track.

32

1 *Can you hear which of them change their sound in the feminine?*

   (a) grand   tall/big   (e) fatigué   tired

   (b) petit   small   (f) chouette   great!/brilliant!

   (c) anglais   English   (g) sage   well behaved

   (d) amusant   amusing   (h) sévère   strict

(i)	intelligent	intelligent		(m)	méchant	nasty
(j)	intéressant	interesting		(n)	bête	silly/stupid
(k)	français	French		(o)	timide	shy
(l)	bavard	talkative		(p)	jeune	young

2 Write out as many of these adjectives in the feminine form as you can.

3 Now make up four short sentences in French, two using feminine words and two masculine, as in this example:

Paul est grand.   Marie est petite.

De quelle couleur? – What colour?

33

Colours are adjectives and must agree with the noun that they describe. Here are some of the most common ones. Listen carefully to the audio to find out which change their *sound*, as well as their *spelling*, in the feminine:

blanc (*f.* blanche)	white	noir(e)	black
bleu(e)	blue	rose	pink
brun(e)	brown	rouge	red
gris(e)	grey	vert(e)	green
jaune	yellow	violet (*f.* violette)	purple

Note that adjectives in French normally come *after* the nouns that they describe, for example:

un crayon rouge   a red pencil

Exercice 5.6

Un jeu de devinettes – A guessing game
Work with a partner. Take it in turns to hide a coloured pencil behind your back. Try to guess which colour your partner has chosen, for example:

C'est un crayon rouge?

– Non.

C'est un crayon jaune?

– Oui.

Exercice 5.7

Look at the objects and describe them, as in the example:

C'est un vélo rose.

Exercice 5.8

Design a poster!

With a partner, design a poster that could be put up in a nursery school classroom to teach young children the French colours, using words and pictures.

Exercice 5.9

Listen to the audio track, then get into groups of four. Practise and perform the conversation.

34

Claire. Sophie, tu as dessin aujourd'hui?

Sophie. Oui. Après la pause de 11 h.

Claire. Tu aimes le nouveau prof de dessin?

Sophie. Ah, oui! Il est super sympa.

Claire. C'est vrai. Malheureusement, je n'ai pas dessin le jeudi. J'ai le latin après la pause. Moi, je trouve que le latin est difficile. Je suis nulle!

Laurent. Cédric, tu trouves ça difficile, le latin?

Cédric. Non, pas tellement. Mais je suis assez fort en langues.

Laurent. Moi, je suis faible en latin. Je préfère les travaux manuels.

Cédric. Moi, c'est pareil. J'aime ça aussi.

super sympa	really nice	moi aussi	me too
que (qu'...)	that (e.g. I find *that* she is strict)	assez fort(e) en	quite good at (e.g. a subject)
nul (*f.* nulle) en	useless at	faible en	poor at/not much good at
ça	it/that (e.g. I find *that* interesting)	c'est pareil	it's the same
pas tellement	not very much	malheureusement	unfortunately

Exercice 5.10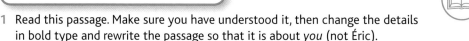

1 Read this passage. Make sure you have understood it, then change the details in bold type and rewrite the passage so that it is about *you* (not Éric).

Je m'appelle Éric. J'ai **treize** ans. Je vais à l'école à **Niort** en **France**. Elle s'appelle **l'École Saint-Agnan**. J'aime bien l'école, parce que j'ai **beaucoup d'amis**. Je mange à la **cantine***. À la cantine, la cuisine est **bonne**! Ma matière préférée, c'est **l'informatique**. Mais j'aime aussi le **latin et l'anglais**. Je suis fort en **maths**; je trouve que le prof est très **sévère**. J'adore le **sport**, mais je suis **nul**!

* la cantine   canteen

2 Try to unscramble these school subjects.

(a) TILNA

(d) STAHM

(b) GLISANA

(e) AEGPLSNO

(c) ETHRISOI

3 Are these sentences true (vrai) or false (faux)? Check Éric's text above.

(a) Éric adore travailler avec des ordinateurs.

(b) Il n'est pas très fort en sport.

(c) Éric va à l'école en Angleterre.

(d) Il prend le déjeuner à la maison.

(e) Éric est nul en maths.

4 Time to spare? Write the correct versions of the 'false' sentences.

Exercice 5.11

Make each adjective feminine if necessary.

1 Claire est (français).

2 Cédric n'est pas (fort) en maths.

3 Nathalie a une amie (bavard) qui s'appelle Anne.

4 Marie lit un livre (intéressant).

5 La maison est (blanc) et (noir).

If you finish early, try these other sentences.

6 Cédric trouve le latin (facile).

7 Anne n'est pas très (intelligent).

8 Ma matière (préféré), c'est la géographie.

9 La prof de dessin, Madame Schmidt, a une voiture (bleu).

10 Mon amie Aurélie est (absent).

Exercice 5.12

It's time for some verb revision.

Write each verb so that it would be correct in the sentence, for example:

In the sentence, He … to the cinema (go/goes/gone), the right word is 'goes'.

If you find these easy, write the whole sentence.

1 Tu n'… pas! (écoute/écoutes/écoutez)

2 Mais ce n'… pas intéressant! (est/es/suis)

3 Claire, tu … un stylo? (a/as/ont)

4 Oui. J'… trois stylos et un crayon dans ma trousse. (ont/avons/ai)

5 Si nous … en classe, le prof n'est pas content. (parlons/parle/parlent)

Les adjectifs (suite) – More about adjectives

35

Some adjectives change their spelling (apart from just adding an e) when forming their feminine.

Adjectives ending in -x end in -se in the feminine:

paresseux	paresseuse	lazy
heureux	heureuse	happy
dangereux	dangereuse	dangerous
joyeux	joyeuse	merry/joyful

Adjectives ending in -f change to -ve in the feminine:

neuf	neuve	brand new
actif	active	active
sportif	sportive	sporty

Adjectives ending in -n change to -nne in the feminine:

ancien	ancienne	old/former

Adjectives ending in -er change to -ère in the feminine:

premier	première	first

There are also adjectives that are used a great deal that simply have to be learned by heart:

Masculine	Feminine	Meaning
beau	belle	handsome/beautiful
gentil	gentille	nice (of a person or an animal)
gros	grosse	big
vieux	vieille	old
long	longue	long
nouveau	nouvelle	new

beau, vieux and nouveau become bel, vieil and nouvel before a vowel or a silent 'h':

Le vieil homme monte dans son bel avion avec son nouvel ami.

Exam style Exercice 5.13 Level 1

Copy these sentences with the adjectives in their correct form.

1 Le garçon est ... (paresseux/paresseuse)

2 La fille est ... (heureux/heureuse)

3 Est-ce que le train est ...? (dangereux/dangereuse)

4 Le professeur est ... (nouveau/nouvel/nouvelle)

5 Ma trousse est ... (neuf/neuve)

Time to spare? Here are some more:

6 Voici mon ... cahier. Il est rouge. (premier/première)

7 Mon père est ... et ma mère est ... (beau/bel/belle)

8 Mon prof de français est ... (grand/grande)

9 Ma grand-mère est ... (vieux/vieil/vieille)

10 Le tableau de la salle de classe est ... (blanc/blanche)

La date, les nombres, les prix

In this chapter we will be looking at dates, numbers and prices.

Mon anniversaire – My birthday

36

For birthdays (les anniversaires), you need to know the numbers up to 31 and the months (les mois).

Les nombres

un/une	1	neuf	9	dix-sept	17	vingt-cinq	25
deux	2	dix	10	dix-huit	18	vingt-six	26
trois	3	onze	11	dix-neuf	19	vingt-sept	27
quatre	4	douze	12	vingt	20	vingt-huit	28
cinq	5	treize	13	vingt et un	21	vingt-neuf	29
six	6	quatorze	14	vingt-deux	22	trente	30
sept	7	quinze	15	vingt-trois	23	trente et un	31
huit	8	seize	16	vingt-quatre	24		

Les mois

janvier	January	juillet	July
février	February	août	August
mars	March	septembre	September
avril	April	octobre	October
mai	May	novembre	November
juin	June	décembre	December

Note that the months in French do not begin with a capital letter.

If your birthday is on the first of a month, you say le premier (the first); for all other dates, you say le deux, le trois and so on. Notice how le premier is abbreviated to le 1er, rather like 'first' is shortened to 1st in English, for example:

Mon anniversaire est le 1er janvier. Et toi?

– Moi, c'est le 23 juillet.

– Et toi? C'est quand, ton anniversaire? Et quelle est la date aujourd'hui?

Exam style Exercice 6.1

Listen to the audio track. When you have heard it, try the exercise below to check your understanding.

37

L'anniversaire de maman

on est quel jour?	what day is it?	un bijoutier	a jeweller
quand	when	un bracelet	a bracelet
acheter	to buy	des boucles	earrings
j'achète	I buy	d'oreille	
l'argent (*m.*)	the money, silver	combien?	how much/
car	for/because		how many?
à *x* kilomètres de	*x* km away from	zut!	bother!
chercher	to look for	trop	too
chez	to/at the house/	cher (*f.* chère)	dear/expensive
	shop of	il faut*	it is necessary
quarante	forty	la carte	the birthday card
cinquante	fifty	d'anniversaire	

1 On which day of the week is maman's birthday?

2 What is Philippe planning to buy for his mother?

3 What does papa think about this?

4 How does the family travel to Belleville?

5 What do they finally buy for maman?

6 At the end of the story, what does Claire suggest that they do next? And what is Philippe's reaction?

* Candidates taking Common Entrance at Level 2 will need to know il faut.   **Level 2**

The French il faut is very useful as it translates a range of expressions, such as 'I must', 'you ought to', 'we should' – the context will normally make clear which. It is followed by an infinitive, for example:

il faut aller à l'école   we must go to school

il faut faire tes devoirs   you've got to do your homework

⬭ Les nombres – Numbers

There are three words for 'number':

le chiffre   figure (digit)

le nombre   number (as in a house or telephone number)

We already know the numbers 1–31. Here are the numbers up to 1000:

quarante	40	quatre-vingt-onze	91
cinquante	50	(4 × 20 + 11)	
soixante	60	quatre-vingt-douze …	92
soixante-dix (60 + 10)	70	quatre-vingt-dix-neuf	99
soixante et onze (60 + 11)	71	cent	100
soixante-douze	72	cent un	101
soixante-treize etc.	73	cent dix	110
up to …		cent vingt et un	121
soixante-dix-neuf	79	deux cents (etc.)	200
(60 + 19)		deux cent trente-deux (etc.)	232
quatre-vingts	80	neuf cent quatre-vingt-	999
quatre-vingt-un	81	dix-neuf	
quatre-vingt-deux etc.,	82	mille	1000
up to …			
quatre-vingt-dix	90		
(4 × 20 + 10)			

Any numbers above 1000 are given in the same order as English:

quatre mille cinq cent neuf   4509

Exercice 6.2

Check above, then write these numbers in figures.

1   quatre

2   vingt-quatre

3   trente-quatre

4   trente-neuf

5   quarante et un

Here are some more for quick finishers.

6   quarante-six

7   cinquante-cinq

8   soixante-treize

9   quatre-vingt-trois

10   quatre-vingt-treize

Exercice 6.3

Now see if you can say these figures out loud in French.

1	44	6	64
2	31	7	75
3	17	8	88
4	39	9	90
5	55	10	94

Les numéros de téléphone – Telephone numbers

38

Telephone numbers in France are always given in groups of two digits at a time. The number 514203, for example, would be given as 51-42-03: cinquante et un, quarante-deux, zéro trois.

When you have had lots of practice with numbers in French and you have listened to these telephone numbers a few times, see if you can read them out. At first, do not hurry.

1	02-51-98-55-05	3	06-76-72-23-15
2	03-49-85-87-89	4	04-33-66-69-79

Vive la différence!

The French way to write figures is slightly different from the British way. In French, a comma is used as a decimal point and a point (full stop) to separate the thousands:

UK	France
3.2	3,2
4,000	4.000 (also written 4 000)

Les verbes: acheter

39

Acheter is a regular -ER verb. Just remember not to worry too much about the accents. Listen carefully to how each part of the verb is pronounced:

acheter: to buy	
j'achète	nous achetons (pronounced ending)
tu achètes	vous achetez (pronounced ending)
il achète	ils achètent
elle achète	elles achètent

In French, quite a few verbs follow this pattern. As you move forward, try to spot the verbs that have these extra accents.

Exam style | Exercice 6.4

1 Look at the picture and give the right price, as in the example:

Les bananes coûtent 1,10 € le kilo.

coûter	to cost	une orange	an orange
la pièce	each	une pomme	an apple
une banane	a banana	une pomme de terre	a potato
une carotte	a carrot	une tomate	a tomato
un melon	a melon		

(a) 2 kilos d'oranges coûtent …

(b) 4 melons coûtent …

(c) 3 kilos de tomates coûtent …

(d) Les carottes coûtent … le kilo.

(e) Les pommes de terre coûtent … le kilo.

(f) Les … et les … coûtent 1,50€ le kilo.

2 Now take it in turns to ask for and to sell the items in the picture, as in the example.

Note that, when talking about a *quantity* of something, we use de, just as we say a kilo **of** bananas in English, for example:

Un kilo de bananes, c'est combien?

– Un euro dix, s'il vous plaît.

Exam style | Exercice 6.5

Checking above, give the right part of acheter for each sentence.

1 Nous ... 2 kilos de carottes. (acheter/achetons/achetez)

2 J'... des pommes de terre et un melon. (achetons/achète/achètes)

3 Elle ... cinq melons. (achètent/achetez/achète)

4 Ils ... des tomates et des pommes. (achète/achètent/achetez)

5 Vous .... des oranges? (achetez/achètes/achète)

Two more important verbs: vouloir and pouvoir

Quand on veut, on peut!

This means, 'when one wants to, one can!' or, in other words, 'where there is a will, there is a way'.

> Reminder: French word on means 'one', but is very often used in French to mean 'we' or 'they', because it has the same verb forms as il and elle, and is therefore easier than nous. It isn't usually added to French verb tables.

The verbs vouloir and pouvoir are rather similar, so we learn them together.

vouloir: to want (to)	
je veu**x**	nous voul**ons**
tu veu**x**	vous voulez
il veut	ils veulent
elle veut	elles veulent

Note the useful phrase: Je veux bien Yes, please/I would like that (and so on).

pouvoir: to be able (to)/can	
je peu**x**	nous pouvons
tu peu**x**	vous pouvez
il peut	ils peuvent
elle peut	elles peuvent

Note that pouvoir followed by an infinitive translates the English 'can', for example:

Je peux venir demain   I *can* come tomorrow.

Exercice 6.6

Check above and give the right part of vouloir for each gap.

1 Tu ... regarder la télé?

2 Je ... écouter la radio.

3 Nous ... manger tout de suite.

4 Elles .... acheter des cadeaux.

5 Vous ... aller en ville?

6 Je ... faire mes devoirs.

7 Papa ... rester à la maison.

8 Maman ... cultiver des roses.

9 Paul et Sylvie ... promener les chiens.

10 ...-vous lire un livre?

Exam style Exercice 6.7

Level 1

Give the right part of the verb shown for each sentence. If you finish quite quickly, try translating the sentences into English.

1 Linda ... acheter une carte pour son ami. (veux/veut/veulent)

2 Elle ne ... pas, parce qu'elle n'a pas d'argent. (peut/peux/pouvons)

3 Philippe et Claire ... chercher un cadeau. (veut/veux/veulent)

4 Ils ne ... pas trouver de cadeau. (peuvent/pouvons/pouvez)

5 Tu ... aller à la piscine? (voulez/veux/veut)

6 Oui, mais je ne ... pas. (peux/peut/pouvez)

Exam style Exercice 6.8

Level 2

Have a go at writing these sentences in French, or at least the *first parts* of each one. Check above as you go for the correct parts of vouloir and pouvoir.

rester	to stay	marché (*m.*)	market
pomme (*f.*)	apple	téléphoner (à ...)	to phone

1 *You (sing.) can eat* at 7.00 p.m.

2 *We are able to watch* the film.

3 *She can stay* at my house.

4 *I can go* to school by train.

5 *They (m.) can buy* some apples in the market.

6 *Where can he read* his book?

7 *Philippe can walk* the dog.

8 *Marie is able to phone* her mother.

9 *Can we* (use on) *watch* the film?

10 *You (pl.) can stay* here if you want.

Exercice 6.9

42

Philippe and Claire carry on with their shopping. Listen to the audio track then choose the correct words to complete the sentences.

1 Philippe wants to buy … (a newspaper/a birthday card/some stamps)

2 There are … to choose from. (many/not many/none)

3 They next go to the … (stationery shop/café/bakery)

4 Philippe needs to borrow … euros from his sister. (two/three/four)

5 Claire … lend him the money. (does/does not/wants to)

Exercice 6.10

Fill in the blanks with words from the box below the paragraph. You will not need every word.

Philippe [1] acheter une carte d'anniversaire pour sa [2]. Mais il ne [3] pas, parce qu'il n'a pas assez d'argent. Il demande à sa sœur s'il peut emprunter trois [4], mais Claire ne peut pas donner les trois euros à son [5]. Elle [6] garder tout son argent pour aller au [7] avec son amie [8].

veut	frère	euros
maman	Aurélie	vélo
veut	peut	cinéma

entrer	to enter	emprunter	to borrow
aller	to go	l'homme (*m.*)	the man
le cinéma	the cinema	prêter	to lend
seulement	only	le marchand de journaux	the newsagent
en face	opposite	la papeterie	the stationer's
demander	to ask	garder	to keep
désolé(e)	sorry	jeune homme	young man
le choix	the choice		

Exercice 6.11

1 Say each of these numbers out loud.

(a) 12	(e) 9	(i) 19	(m) 36
(b) 2	(f) 3	(j) 10	(n) 7
(c) 11	(g) 13	(k) 6	(o) 17
(d) 1	(h) 23	(l) 16	

2 Write these prices in figures, for example:

trois euros vingt   320€

(a) dix euros quarante

(b) trente-deux euros

(c) sept euros dix-sept

(d) quatre-vingt-treize euros quatre-vingt-dix-neuf

(e) deux cents euros vingt-cinq

Exercice 6.12

Au marché – **At the market**

Imagine a fruit and vegetable market for one minute and then take it in turns to see how many of the items you can remember in French!

Who will come up with the longest shopping list?

Tu es comment?

In this chapter we learn how to describe ourselves and other people. We learn about colours and clothes, and more about adjectives.

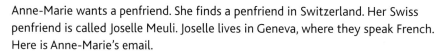

Exercice 7.1

43

Read this introduction, then try the exercise.

Anne-Marie wants a penfriend. She finds a penfriend in Switzerland. Her Swiss penfriend is called Joselle Meuli. Joselle lives in Geneva, where they speak French. Here is Anne-Marie's email.

As you look at Anne-Marie's email, listen to the audio track. Notice how emails are set out in French and what sort of expressions are used:

De: ambenoit@ …

À: joselle@ …

Objet: Bonjour

Bonjour Joselle,

Tu veux être ma nouvelle correspondante? Je suis contente! J'aime la Suisse, surtout le lac de Genève: ici on dit 'Le lac Léman'!. J'ai 12 ans et j'habite à La Roche-sur-Yon depuis 8 ans.

J'ai les cheveux bruns et longs et les yeux bleus. Je suis assez grande (je mesure 1 m 53) et je suis sportive. J'aime aussi la musique. Mes amies disent que je suis souriante et optimiste!

Voilà! Et toi? Tu es comment? Écris-moi vite!

Amicalement,

Anne-Marie Benoît

Envoyé de la tablette de A-M. Benoît

---

un(e) correspondant(e)	a penfriend (*m./f.*)	depuis	since
la Suisse	Switzerland	depuis 8 ans	for 8 years
surtout	especially	les cheveux	hair
le lac Léman	Lake Geneva	les yeux	eyes

mesurer	to measure	souriant(e)	cheerful
sportif (*f.* sportive)	sporty	optimiste	optimistic
(ils/elles) disent	(they) say	tu es comment?	what are you like?

Choose the correct word from the selection below to fill each gap. You will have three words left over.

1 Joselle habite en …

2 Anne-Marie a … ans.

3 Joselle est la … correspondante d'Anne-Marie.

4 Genève est située … d'un lac.

5 Le lac … lac Léman.

| douze | deux | nouveau | Suisse |
| nouvelle | s'appelle | à côté | France |

La description

Elle est comment, Julie?

Elle a 15 ans. Elle est anglaise. Elle a les cheveux longs. Elle est assez grande, assez mince, mais pas trop maigre.

Before we begin to describe ourselves in French, we need to learn how some expressions are a little different from their English equivalents.

To give your age, you say:

j'ai 12 ans (using the verb avoir)

To give your height, you say:

je mesure 1 m 53 (using the verb mesurer)

To give the colour of your eyes or describe your hair, you say:

j'ai les yeux verts (adding the word les)

j'ai les cheveux longs (adding the word les)

Moi, je suis … (Describing people)

Je suis …	I am …		
aimable	friendly	drôle	funny
honnête	honest	poli(e)	polite
beau (*f.* belle)	good-looking	généreux (*f.* généreuse)	generous
joli(e)	pretty	souriant(e)	cheerful
dingue	crazy	gentil (*f.* gentille)	pleasant
mignon (*f.* mignonne)	cute	sympa(thique)	nice

Et mon apparence physique? – What about my appearance?

Je suis …	I am …		
bronzé(e)	tanned	maigre	thin, skinny
grand(e)	tall	fort(e)	strong
costaud	well-built	mince	slim
gros(se)	big/large	je mesure x mètres	I am *x* metres tall
de taille moyenne	of medium build	je pèse x kilos	I weigh *x* kilos

Et mes cheveux? – And my hair?

j'ai les cheveux …	my hair is …		
blancs	white	noirs	black
frisés	frizzy	bruns	brown
blonds	blonde	roux	red, ginger
longs	long	châtains	mid-brown
bouclés	curly	raides	straight
		courts	short

> Reminder: These are shown in the masculine plural, to agree with cheveux.

Like blond(e), châtain is also used to describe people who have that colour hair: elle est châtain. Note also the special word for red (roux) when referring to hair. If you have very little hair or none at all, you are chauve (bald)!

Exercice 7.2

Listen to these conversations on the audio track *before* you read them through. When you have studied them carefully with your teacher, you could practise and perform them. Use the vocabulary below to help you.

Dialogue 1

44

Philippe.	Cédric! Tu as vu le nouveau venu?
Cédric.	Non. Il est comment?
Philippe.	Il est assez costaud, pas très grand mais fort.
Cédric.	Un peu comme Léon?
Philippe.	Oui. Et très sportif. Il fait du ski!
Cédric.	Ça alors! Il a quel âge?
Philippe.	Quatorze ans, je crois.

Dialogue 2

45

Anne-Marie.	Tiens! Salut Claire!
Claire.	Salut! J'ai une lettre de ma nouvelle correspondante!
Anne-Marie.	Ah, bon! Où est-ce qu'elle habite?
Claire.	En Allemagne.
Anne-Marie.	Et elle est comment?
Claire.	Elle est blonde, très grande, sportive. Elle fait du cheval dans la Forêt Noire!
Anne-Marie.	Chouette!

tu as vu	you have seen	comme	like
le nouveau venu	the new guy	chouette!	brilliant/cool!
je crois	I think	ça alors!	really!
tiens!	well, well!		

Exercice 7.3

Draw each person based on their description.

1 Il est très petit. Il a les cheveux roux et frisés. Il a 3 ans.

2 Elle est assez grosse. Elle a les cheveux verts et les yeux noirs!

3 Bobby a les cheveux longs et roux. Il a 16 ans. Il est grand et mince.

69

Exercice 7.4

Les vêtements – **Clothes**

1 Study the clothes for one minute. Then close your book and try to describe the items to your partner. Don't forget to mention the colours of each item, for example:

le jean est bleu/il y a un jean bleu

- ■ un T-shirt
- ■ un short
- ■ un jean
- ■ un pull
- ■ un pantalon
- ■ une jupe
- ■ une robe
- ■ une chemise
- ■ un chapeau
- ■ des lunettes
- ■ des chaussures
- ■ des baskets

2 Qu'est-ce que tu portes aujourd'hui?   What are you wearing today?

Now have a conversation with your partner, describing what you are each wearing, for example:

Je porte un pantalon noir et un pull bleu.

Exercice 7.5

46

Listen to the audio track as you read the passage.

Sara et Nathalie entrent dans une boutique de mode, qui se trouve à un kilomètre de chez Nathalie, au centre-ville. Nathalie a une amie, Véronique, qui travaille à la boutique le samedi et pendant les vacances. Le père de Véronique est le propriétaire de la boutique. Véronique a 14 ans. Nathalie a 13 ans mais son anniversaire est dans trois jours. Son amie est de taille moyenne. Elle a les cheveux roux et bouclés et les yeux verts. Les deux copines adorent s'habiller à la mode!

Nathalie économise: tous les dimanches elle met un peu d'argent de côté pour acheter des vêtements. Maintenant elle a 50 euros et elle peut acheter une robe qu'elle peut porter le jour de son anniversaire.

With your teacher, using the vocabulary below, go through the passage above to make sure you understand it. Do a little at a time.

la boutique	the shop	économiser	to save up
le copain	the friend (*m.*)	la ville	the town; the city
à la mode	in fashion	mettre de côté	to put aside
la copine	the friend (*f.*)	le propriétaire	the owner
se trouver	to be situated		

See if you can spot the French expressions for:

1 ... which is situated one kilometre away from ...

2 ... in the town centre

3 ... who works in the shop

4 ... in the holidays

5 ... on Saturdays

Exam style | Exercice 7.6

 Level 1

Give the right French verb shown in brackets.

1 Marc n'... pas aller dans les magasins. (aime/aiment/aimes)

2 Marc et Claude ... de la musique. (parlent/parles/parlez)

3 Le samedi, Véronique ... en ville. (vont/vais/va)

4 Ses parents ... propriétaires d'une boutique. (sont/ont/font)

5 Nathalie ne ... pas acheter une robe. (pouvez/peux/peut)

Exam style | Exercice 7.7

Match up the sentence halves so they make the best sense.

1 Nathalie travaille
2 Tu veux aller
3 Après le petit-déjeuner,
4 Claude achète quatre
5 Sara et Marc mangent

(a) les croissants de maman.
(b) billets d'entrée.
(c) au centre-ville le samedi.
(d) je vais à la boutique.
(e) au cinéma ce soir?

Exercice 7.8

Write a short description in French for each picture. Give at least one detail about the hair and one about the clothing for each, for example:

Sonia est châtain. Elle porte un T-shirt bleu.

■ Chantal

■ Marie-Claire

■ Sylvie

■ Guy

■ Carl

■ Jean-Michel

Exam style | Exercice 7.9

Level 2

Describe yourself by writing an email of 80 to 120 words.

If you're writing to a boy, start with Cher or, if it's a girl, Chère. You must mention at least **four** of the following:

● où tu habites — where you live
● les environs — the area round where you live
● combien tu mesures — your height

- tes cheveux   your hair
- tes activités préférées   your favourite pastimes.

Making adjectives plural

You will see as you go on that most plural adjectives end in s. Some end in x and a few don't change at all:

s: x:

les filles heureuses   the happy girls   les beaux avions   the beautiful aeroplanes

No change:

des garçons sympa   some nice boys

Finally, note that some adjectives do not change at all in the feminine or the plural, for example:

marron   reddish-brown   super   brilliant
cool   cool   sympa   nice

le garçon est super   les garçons sont super
la fille est super   les filles sont super

Position of adjectives

Normally, adjectives in French come after the noun they describe, but a few generally come before. Here are some to look out for:

grand(e)   petit(e)   beau (belle)
nouveau (nouvelle)   vieux (vieille)   joli(e)
gentil(le)   bon(ne)   long(ue)

Here is a little acronym that you can learn to memorise the adjectives that come before their nouns:

B   Beauty   beau, joli, vilain

A   Age   jeune, vieux/vieille

G   Goodness   bon, mauvais, méchant

S   Size   grand, petit, haut, gros

Exam style | Exercice 7.10

Listen to the audio track, then attempt the questions to see how much you have understood. Use the vocabulary box to help you.

1 What is Nathalie wearing?

2 What is Marc wearing?

3 How do we know Nathalie's top is new?

4 What does Sara say about it?

5 What does the skating rink employee ask them first?

6 How much money does the employee ask them for?

pendant	during	quelle pointure chaussez-vous?	what size shoes do you take?
louer	to hire		
les vacances	the holidays	une écharpe	a scarf
les patins	the skates	deux fois	two times/twice
faire du patinage	to go skating	foncé	dark (of colours)
la patinoire	the skating rink	le guichet	desk, counter
vous êtes combien?	how many are you?		
on est quatre	there are four of us		
porter	to wear		

Exercice 7.11

Read the conversation as you listen to the audio track, then try the exercise below.

Nathalie et Sara se trouvent devant la boutique de Véronique.

Nathalie.   Oh! Regarde cette jolie robe rouge! Mais elle coûte 85 euros!

Sara.   Oui, elle est belle, mais elle est chère. Tu as combien d'argent?

Nathalie.   Cinquante euros. Tiens! Voilà Véronique!

Sara.   Nathalie veut acheter cette robe, mais elle est trop chère.

Véronique.   Pas de problème! Les soldes commencent aujourd'hui!

Nathalie.   Ah! Les soldes! Super!

Véronique.   Je demande à papa le prix de cette robe avec la remise!

Nathalie.	D'accord.
Véronique.	Il dit que c'est 60 euros …
Nathalie.	Zut …!
Véronique.	Mais pour toi, il fait un prix spécial! Tu peux avoir la robe pour 45 euros!
Nathalie.	Chouette! Merci beaucoup, Véronique!

In the text, find the French for these expressions.

1 outside the shop *or* in front of the shop

2 it costs

3 how much money?

4 no problem

5 the sales

6 the reduction

7 okay

8 great!

Exercice 7.12

Draw the people described below. Don't worry about artistic skill; just show you have understood!

1 Elle est grande et elle a les cheveux longs et noirs. Elle porte une robe violette, un T-shirt bleu et un chapeau rouge.

2 Il est petit et gros. Il a les cheveux courts et frisés. Il porte un vieux pantalon et des baskets vertes.

3 Mon ami Philippe a les cheveux blonds et courts, le visage* bronzé et il mesure 1 m 75. Il est mince, sportif et il porte des vêtements cool!

* le visage   the face

 # Ma famille et mes animaux

Families can be big or small, simple or complicated. And they include our animals too!

Exercice 8.1

49

Listen to the audio track and complete the activity below.

que	that/which	le grand-père	the grandfather
formidable	wonderful	notre	our (+ *singular noun*)
le père	the father		
handicapé(e)	disabled	la grand-mère**	the grandmother
la mère	the mother	mes grands-parents	my grandparents
adopté(e)	adopted		
la sœur*	the sister	nos	our (+ *plural noun*)
japonais(e)	Japanese	s'occuper de	to look after
le frère	the brother	le morceau de musique	piece, piece of music, 'track'
d'origine …	of … origin		

* The o and e of diphthongs, as in the word sœur, are traditionally joined together in printed books.

**Although 'grandmother' is feminine, the grand does not have a feminine ending; the plural is les grands-mères.

Complete these sentences in French:

1 Tochiko habite à … (La Roche-sur-Yon/La Rochelle/Rochefort)

2 Cette ville est … (en Vendée/en vente/dans le Vercors)

3 Les frères de Tochiko … le sport. (adorent/détestent/jouent)

4 Marie-Christine adore … et … (la musique/le dessin/la géographie)

5 Mina a … ans. (sept/huit/neuf)

Une sœur qui s'appelle ... – A sister called ...

In English, we can say 'a sister called Sophie'.

In French, we *must* say a sister who is called Sophie, by putting in the word qui: une sœur qui s'appelle Sophie.

J'adore le sport – I love sport

Another little difference between French and English is that we cannot say 'I like (sport etc.)'; we have to say 'I like *the* sport', when we mean something generally, like all sport.

Here are a few examples. You will be able to make up lots of your own!

j'aime la musique classique	I like classical music
je déteste le poisson	I hate fish
Marie adore les chevaux	Marie loves horses

Exercice 8.2

Give the English for these expressions.

1 le père de Michel

2 les grands-mères d'Olivier

3 la sœur de Marie-Christine

4 la mère de Mina

5 le grand-père de Christine

Exercice 8.3

50

1 Listen to the audio track, then answer the questions to show your understanding.

la récré	break time	un(e) voisin(e)	a neighbour
nombreux (*f.* nombreuse)	numerous	incroyable	incredible
une famille nombreuse	a big family	aîné(e)	eldest/elder
en fait	in fact, by the way	cadet(te)	youngest, younger
on est sept	there are seven of us	la gendarmerie	the police
on a	we have		

(a) How many people does Mina say are in her family?

(b) Who lives nearby?

(c) How many bedrooms are there in Mina's house?

(d) What does Mina's younger brother want to be?

(e) Who is Marie-Christine?

2 Now describe your own family. Here are some more words to help you:

le mari	the husband	la fille	the daughter; the girl
la femme	the wife; the woman	la petite-fille	the granddaughter
un oncle	an uncle	le petit-fils	the grandson
une tante	an aunt	les petits-enfants	the grandchildren
le neveu	the nephew	un demi-frère	a half/stepbrother
la nièce	the niece	une demi-sœur	a half/stepsister
le cousin	the cousin (*m.*)	un beau-père	a father-in-law/stepfather
la cousine	the cousin (*f.*)	une belle-mère	a mother-in-law/stepmother
le fils	the son		

Exercice 8.4

1 True or false? Read each sentence carefully then write V for vrai (true) or F for faux (false).

(a) Mon oncle est la sœur de ma tante.

(b) Ma belle-mère est la mère de mon père.

(c) Mes grands-parents sont les parents de mes parents.

(d) Ma cousine est la petite-fille de mon oncle et de ma tante.

(e) Ma tante est la sœur de mon père ou de ma mère.

2 Draw up a family tree for the family described here.

Je m'appelle Sonia. J'ai un frère qui s'appelle Guy et une sœur qui s'appelle Marina. Mes parents s'appellent Jean-Jacques et Sandrine. Les parents de maman sont Alphonse et Léopoldine et mes autres* grands-parents sont François et Marie-Claude. Et bien, voilà!

* autre   other

Exam style   Exercice 8.5

Level 2

Role play

A is staying with a French family and arrives at their house.

Take it in turns to be A and B (one of the parents). B begins.

A.	B.
	Bonjour et bienvenue chez nous!
Hello B. Thank you.	Ça va? Pas trop fatigué(e)?
No, I'm fine.	C'est bien …
Where is André?	Il arrive. Il va chercher* sa sœur à l'école.
Does André have a brother?	Mais oui! Et deux sœurs!
	Tu as des frères ou des sœurs?

[?]

* Il va chercher He's fetching

Exercice 8.6

Looking at the pictures, say one animal that you have at home and one that you *do not* have, as in this example:

Moi, j'ai un chien à la maison, mais je n'ai pas de chat.

> Reminder: Always use pas de to say we do not have something or there isn't something.

Les animaux – Animals

- un chien

- un chat

- un lapin

- un cheval

- un poisson

- un oiseau

- un âne

- un hamster

- une araignée

- une vache

- une souris

- une tortue

Note the following plurals:

| un cheval | des chevaux |
| un oiseau | des oiseaux |

Exercice 8.7

51

Listen to the audio track, then answer the questions.

1 What does Tochiko ask Philippe about his dog?

2 Who lives with Philippe?

3 Why is having a dog not easy for them?

Les questions – Questions

52

There are three ways of asking a question in French:

1 Inversion (don't forget the hyphen!)

Here, we take the verb phrase and turn it round or invert it:

Statement	Tu as des animaux.	You have some animals.
Question	**As-tu** des animaux?	**Have you** any animals?

> Reminder: Sometimes, to make the language flow more easily, we have to put in the letter t:
>
> | | |
> |---|---|
> | il aime | he likes |
> | aime-t-il? | does he like? |
> | elle a | she has |
> | a-t-elle? | does she have? |

2 Est-ce que/Est-ce qu' (before a vowel)

Statement	Tu aimes le chocolat.	You like chocolate.
Question	**Est-ce que** tu aimes le chocolat?	Do you like chocolate?
Statement	Il aime la géographie.	He likes geography.
Question	**Est-ce qu'**il aime la géographie?	Does he like geography?

Here we place the phrase est-ce que before the verb. Note that est-ce que becomes est-ce qu' before a vowel or silent 'h'.

3 Use your tone of voice, rising at the end

Statement	Tu vas au cinéma.	You are going to the cinema.
Question	Tu vas au cinéma?	Are you going to the cinema?

Exercice 8.8

Discuss these sentences with your teacher, or decide in groups what they mean.

1 Aimes-tu ton école?

2 Est-ce que les profs parlent anglais?

3 Nous allons à Paris cet après-midi?

4 Est-ce que tu aimes mon petit village?

5 Vous détestez les maths?

6 Habites-tu avec ta grand-mère?

7 Est-ce que tu peux manger une tartine?

8 Est-ce qu'Olivier va chez sa tante?

9 Est-ce que nous arrivons à Nantes à 13 h?

10 Le train arrive à Paris à 14 h?

Exercice 8.9

Try saying or writing these examples in French. Start with the one on the left, then make it a question, like the ones on the right.

For example : **You (*sing.*) watch TV.**   **Do you watch TV?**
                Tu regardes la télé.   Est-ce que tu regardes la télé?

1 You (*sing.*) are French.   Are you French?

2 You (*sing.*) live in France.   Do you live in France?

3 You (*sing.*) like (the) school.   Do you like school?

4 The teachers are nice.   Are the teachers nice?

5 You (*sing.*) eat croissants.   Do you eat croissants?

Exercice 8.10

Now see if you can use the following pictures as prompts to ask your partner some questions, for example:

Est-ce que tu aimes les ordinateurs?

The questions may be as simple as you like or as detailed!

◯ Les verbes: écrire

Here is the verb écrire ('to write').

écrire: to write	
j'écris	nous écrivons
tu écris	vous écrivez
il écrit	ils écrivent
elle écrit	elles écrivent

Reminder: Each French verb you have met means *two* English ones, for example nous écrivons means 'we write' *or* 'we are writing'.

Can you give the two English meanings of all the other parts of écrire?

Finally, we use à with écrire, to say we write *to* people, just as we do in English.

Exam style Exercice 8.11

Level 2

Translate these sentences.

1 Marie is writing to her grandmother.   écrire, grand-mère (*f.*)

2 We write to our pen friends.   écrire, correspondant(e) (*m./f.*)

3 I am writing in my exercise book.   écrire, cahier (*m.*)

4 They (*f.*) are writing a letter to Nicolas.   écrire, lettre (*f.*)

5 Antoine and Françoise are writing emails.   écrire, e-mail (*m.*)

Reminder: Remember to say 'some' emails.

Exercice 8.12

Make the verbs in these sentences negative.

1 Marie **aime** écrire à sa grand-mère.

2 La sœur de François **mange** à la cantine de l'école.

3 Nous **rentrons** à la maison.

4 Antoine et Chantal **écrivent** aujourd'hui.

5 Tu **peux** regarder la télévision après le dîner.

6 Le frère aîné de Christine **s'appelle** Jérôme.

7 Tochiko **veut manger** au restaurant ce soir.

8 L'oncle de Jules **est** très poli.

Exercice 8.13

Working in pairs or groups, separate the words and rewrite this passage in normal sentences. Translate as much as you can into English.

> Reminder: Proper names will need capital letters.

jenesuispasanglaisjesuis

françaisjhabiteànantesav

ecmesdeuxfrèresetmas

soeurnousavonsdeuxpetits

chiensquisappellentbalzacet

tiggyetunchatquisappelletu

rcetquialesyeuxbleus

Exercice 8.14

Listen to the audio track as you read the passage. Then do the exercises.

Les magasins à Nantes sont super. Il y a de bons magasins à La Roche-sur-Yon, mais je préfère Nantes parce qu'il y a un plus grand choix. Par exemple, il y a un magasin qui s'appelle 'Nos Amis les Animaux' où on trouve des chiots, des chatons et des hamsters. À Nantes, il y a des chiens, des chats, des hamsters, mais aussi des cochons d'Inde, des oiseaux, des poissons rouges et beaucoup d'autres animaux.

Aurélie, 10 ans, Belleville (Vendée)

| le magasin | the shop | le chaton | the kitten |
| plus grand | bigger | le chiot | the puppy |

Choose the option that makes the best sense.

1 Un chiot est un petit … (chien/chat/hamster)

2 Un chaton est un petit … (chien/chat/hamster)

Now answer these questions in French.

3 Aurélie préfère les magasins de quelle ville?

4 Comment s'appelle le magasin d'animaux à La Roche-sur-Yon?

Exercice 8.15

Work in pairs. Talk about your families and your pets, as in the example:

Vous êtes combien dans la famille?

– On est trois. Ma mère, mon père et moi.

– Tu as des animaux?

– Oui, j'ai un chien et deux chats.

8   *Ma famille et mes animaux*

On se retrouve!

In this chapter, we shall look at arranging to meet and at places to go. There are some new verbs, and we shall also look at a simple way of talking about the future.

Qu'est-ce qu'on fait demain?

On va au cinéma?

Bonne idée!

55

Listen to the audio track, then answer the questions below in English.

on se retrouve	let's meet	se retrouver	to meet up
on fait quoi?	what shall we do?	on se retrouve où?	where shall we meet?
demain	tomorrow	la patinoire	the skating rink
au cinéma	to the cinema	un arrêt de bus	a bus stop
une idée	an idea	la rue	the street
ça marche	good idea, OK	à demain	see you tomorrow

1 Where does Claire first suggest they go?

2 What's on at the cinema?

3 What time does it start?

4 Where is the bus stop?

5 When will they meet there?

À, au, aux

56

In French, the same words are used for saying *to the* (something) as *at the* (something). This is because à means both 'to' and 'at'.

When using à, note that à + le shortens to au and à + les becomes aux. As you will see in the examples, à + la (feminine) does not change.

Look at these examples.

Feminine singular

| On va à la piscine. | We go **to the** swimming pool. |
| On est à la plage. | We are **at the** beach. |

Masculine singular

| On va au parc. | We go **to the** park. |
| On est au théâtre. | We are **at the** theatre. |

Singular before a vowel (masculine or feminine)

| On va à l'église (*f.*) | We go **to the** church. |
| On est à l'aéroport (*m.*) | We are **at the** airport. |

Plural (masculine or feminine)

| On va aux magasins. | We go **to the** shops. |
| On est aux écuries. | We are **at the** stables. |

Exercice 9.2

Write the English for the phrases *in italics*.

1 On se retrouve *au café*.

2 Paul et Maurice mangent *au restaurant*.

3 Il y a un bon film *au cinéma Concorde*.

Here are some more for early finishers.

6 Nous n'allons pas *aux écuries*.

7 On prend le bus pour aller *à l'église*.

8 Le film commence *au cinéma* à vingt et une heures.

4 Anne ne va pas *à l'église*.

5 Claire et Paul vont *au Café des Sports*.

9 Papa arrive *à l'aéroport* à seize heures trente.

10 Il retrouve maman *au parc*.

Exercice 9.3

Write in French. These are quite tricky and need careful thought!

1 to the café

2 to the cafés

3 to his brother

4 to Claire

5 to Philippe's uncle

6 at the swimming pool

7 at the bus stop (arrêt (*m.*) de bus)

8 to the cinema

9 to the restaurant

10 at home

Exercice 9.4

Look at the pictures. Work in pairs. Make up a conversation like the one in this example:

On se retrouve où?

– À la piscine.

– À quelle heure?

– À sept heures.

– D'accord. À la piscine à sept heures. Au revoir.

■ la piscine

■ la discothèque

■ le restaurant

■ l'école

■ le marché

■ l'église

J'ai faim! – I'm hungry!

57

The French for 'to be hungry' is avoir faim (to have hunger):

Exercice 9.5

58

Listen to the audio track and read the dialogue.

Josette.	Bonjour.
Daniel.	Bonjour. Comment t'appelles-tu?
Josette.	Je m'appelle Josette. Et toi?
Daniel.	Moi, je m'appelle Daniel.
Josette.	Qu'est ce que tu vas faire?
Daniel.	Je vais aller à la pêche.
Josette.	Tu vas pêcher des poissons?
Daniel.	Oui. Je vais pêcher de gros poissons.

Plus tard, à la maison

Josette.	Il y a un petit garçon qui s'appelle Daniel.
Maman.	Ah bon …
Josette.	Il va pêcher de gros poissons!
Maman.	Ah bon …
Josette.	Moi, avec Daniel, nous allons chercher des serpents!
Maman.	Ah bon …

aller à la pêche	to go fishing
fais voir!	let's have a look!
un poisson	a fish
pêcher un poisson	to catch a fish
un serpent	a snake

1 What does Daniel say he's going to do?

2 What does Josette say to her mother first?

3 What does Josette's mother say that shows she is not really listening?

4 What does Josette then say to shock her mother?

Exam style | Exercice 9.6

Match the sentence halves. Say which number goes with which letter.

1 Qu'est-ce qu'on
2 On peut aller au
3 Tu veux aller à la
4 Le film commence à
5 On se retrouve à l'

(a) piscine?
(b) huit heures et demie.
(c) arrêt de bus.
(d) fait après le petit-déjeuner?
(e) restaurant?

If you finish early, translate the full sentences into English.

Exercice 9.7

Decode these destinations!

Each one is a phrase containing au, à la, or aux. You will need five of these words.

parc	café	théâtre	piscine	patinoire
cinéma		magasins	club	restaurant

1 aémucina
2 palàcinesi
3 untaersaratu

4 féauac
5 acpura

Exercice 9.8

Write these sentences in French.

1 At the church (église (f.)).
2 Do you want to go fishing?
3 After school.   (after *the* school!)
4 Let's meet.   (the title of the chapter!)
5 Where shall we meet? (the title of the chapter + the word for 'where')
6 At the bus stop.
7 The film starts (commencer).
8 At what time?

Le futur proche – What is going to happen

The futur proche tense expresses what *is going to* happen in the *future*. This tense is expressed in French by using the verb aller followed by an infinitive – which is exactly what we do in English:

Present   **Future**

je mange   I eat, I am eating   je **vais** manger   I **am going** to eat

We could set out all the possible parts of manger using the futur proche, as follows:

je vais manger   nous allons manger

tu vas manger   vous allez manger

il va manger   ils vont manger

elle va manger   elles vont manger

Notice that manger doesn't change its spelling. Plus, you have already learned aller, so there is actually nothing new to learn!

Note the position of ne and pas in the negative forms:

je ne vais pas manger   I am not going to eat

tu ne vas pas manger   you are not going to eat

... and so on.

Exercice 9.9

Rewrite these expressions in the futur proche, so that, for example, *you sing* (tu chantes) becomes *you are going to sing*.

> Reminder: There are *two* things to do here:
>
> First, put the right part of aller: Tu vas ...
>
> Second, make the verb infinitive (chantes becomes chanter): Tu vas chanter.

1   Tu trouves   6   Maman écoute

2   Nous regardons   7   Nous habitons

3   Elle mange   8   Paul donne

4   Il chante   9   Vous achetez

5   Je chante   10 Nous achetons

Exercice 9.10

Using the notes on the futur proche to help you, try writing these sentences in French. Of course, you will need aller throughout.

1 I'm going to watch the television. regarder

2 She's going to speak to the boy. parler, garçon (*m.*)

3 He is going to go to church on Sundays. église (*f.*)

4 He is not going to go to school on Saturdays. école (*f.*)

5 She's not going to listen. écouter

6 Is Daniel going to go to the swimming pool? piscine (*f.*)

7 Is Josette going to look for snakes? chercher, serpent (*m.*)

8 What are we going to do? faire

9 Do you want to go to the café? vouloir, café (*m.*)

10 What time are we going to eat? heure (*f.*), aller, manger

Exercice 9.11

Which sentence is the odd one out and why?

1 J'adore les sciences, surtout la chimie.

2 Moi, j'aime la géographie. C'est passionnant!

3 Je suis sportif. J'aime les cours de gymnastique.

4 J'adore les bananes. Et tous les autres fruits!

5 Moi, j'aime beaucoup le latin. C'est fascinant.

passionnant(e)	exciting	la gymnastique	gymnastics
le cours	lesson, class	fascinant(e)	fascinating

Exam style Exercice 9.12

Level 2

Write an email of 80 to 120 words, in which you say what you (and your friends) are going to do over the weekend. You must mention four of the following:

● vendredi – cinéma Friday – cinema

● samedi – jouer au squash Saturday – playing squash

● samedi soir – restaurant Saturday evening – restaurant

● dimanche – piscine Sunday – swimming pool

● ce week-end this weekend

● un problème* a problem*

* For the 'problem', say you cannot go to lunch on Sunday because you are going to the beach.

10 Les loisirs

In this chapter, we shall look at some of the things people like to do in their free time. There are also two new verb groups to learn.

Qu'est-ce que tu fais à la maison après les cours?

Moi, je joue au ping-pong avec ma sœur ou bien je joue au tennis.

Quelquefois je dessine ou j'écoute de la musique. Et toi?

Exam style Exercice 10.1

59

parfois   sometimes

gagner   to win

venir   to come

Listen to the audio track and add the right words to complete the sentences.

1 Marcel plays … with his sister. (hockey/table tennis/golf)

2 He wins … (always/sometimes/never)

3 This afternoon Marcel is doing his … (English/maths/homework)

4 Henri asks if Philippe wants to go to … (his house/Marcel's house/the cinema)

5 Marcel has to … (do his homework/help his parents/tidy his room)

◯ Les verbes du deuxième groupe – Second-group verbs (-IR)

60

So far, most of the verbs you have met have either been -ER (first-group) verbs, or else they have been unlike any others (we call

92

these 'irregular'). We are now going to meet a second verb group: -IR (second-group) verbs. Rather like -ER (first-group) verbs, these verbs follow a pattern of endings that the other verbs in the group share.

Note that venir, used in the previous audio exercise, is irregular – it is *not* a second-group verb.

The verbs in this group all follow the pattern of finir. Just like for -ER verbs, the **stem** never changes but the **endings** do. Every verb in the group changes in the same way. The endings are shown in **bold**:

finir: to finish	
je fini**s**	nous finissons
tu fini**s**	vous finissez
il fini**t**	ils finissent
elle fini**t**	elles finissent

So because we know that the verb punir (to punish) is a second-group verb, we can use punir with the same endings as finir, for example:

nous finissons   we finish

therefore:

nous punissons   we punish

... and so on.

Exercice 10.2

1 Write out *one* of these verbs in full, checking carefully the endings set out above.

(a) choisir   to choose

(b) remplir   to fill

(c) punir   to punish

2 Now give the endings for the gaps in the sentences below.

(a) La mère pun... sa fille.

(b) Philippe pun... le chien.

(c) Pourquoi pun...- tu ta sœur?

(d) Je ne pun... pas mes enfants.

(e) Le professeur pun... la classe.

(f) Nous ne pun... pas les animaux.

Exam style | Exercice 10.3

Complete these sentences with the correct form of the verb from the brackets.

1 Tu ... tes devoirs? (finis/finit/finissons)

2 Elle ... un gâteau. (choisis/choisissez/choisit)

3 Nous ... les verres. (remplit/remplissent/remplissons)

4 Ils ... les élèves. (punit/punissent/punissez)

5 On ... le déjeuner. (finis/finit/finissez)

6 Elle ne ... pas la fille. (punis/punissent/punit)

7 On ... un cadeau pour maman. (choisit/choisis/choisissent)

8 Tu ... mon verre, s'il te plaît. (remplissez/remplit/remplis)

9 Vous ne ... pas un CD? (choisissez/choisissons/choisissent)

10 Je ne ... pas mon chien. (punit/punissons/punis)

Exam style | Exercice 10.4

Level 2

Write these sentences in French. Use the words provided to help you. If you finish quite quickly, make up some of your own, using the -IR verbs you have already met.

1 He chooses a present.   choisir, cadeau (*m.*)

2 I fill your glass.   remplir, verre (*m.*)

3 You (*sing.*) punish the pupil.   punir, élève

4 They (*f.*) finish the homework.   finir, devoirs (*m.pl.*)

5 We (on) choose our breakfast.   choisir

6 You (*pl.*) don't finish the homework.

7 I don't choose my lunch.

8 Does she punish the pupils?

9 Do they (*f.*) finish the homework?

10 You (*sing.*) fill his glass.

○ Les loisirs – Leisure activities (using jouer and faire)

To talk about the things we do (or are going to do) in our free time, we often use the two verbs jouer and faire.

1 jouer (to play) is followed by au (*m.*), à la (*f.*) or aux (*pl.*), before the noun for the sport, which could be masculine, feminine, singular or plural.

2 faire (to do) is used in French where in English there is a variety of expressions like 'go', for example 'go cycling', 'go for a walk' and so on.

■ Marcel et Anne-Marie jouent au tennis

■ Sabine et sa sœur font du ski

jouer **au** football (*m.*)	to play football	faire un tour	to go around (a place)
jouer **au** tennis (*m.*)	to play tennis	faire une promenade	to go for a walk
jouer **au** rugby (*m.*)	to play rugby	faire du vélo/du cyclisme	to go cycling
jouer **aux** boules (*pl.*)	to play boules	faire du ski	to go skiing
jouer **aux** échecs (*pl.*)	to play chess	faire de l'équitation	to go horse-riding

> Reminder: While jouer is a first-group verb, faire is irregular. In case you need to refresh your memory, here it is in full again:

faire: to do/to make	
je fais	nous faisons
tu fais	vous faites
il fait	ils font
elle fait	elles font

Exercice 10.5

Qu'est-ce que tu fais après les cours? – **What do you do after school?**

Can you give in French a few of the activities you do after school?

Exam style | Exercice 10.6

Match the sentence halves.

1	Pourquoi ne vas-tu pas	(a)	fais du vélo.
2	Michel et Sonia	(b)	joue au rugby.
3	Philippe	(c)	jouer au tennis ce soir?
4	Je vais faire	(d)	font une promenade.
5	Après les cours je	(e)	un tour de Paris.

Exercice 10.7

1 Using the last exercise to help you, think whether you would use jouer or faire in each of these sentences.

(a) Monsieur Blériot … au tennis avec son amie.

(b) Madame Colette … une promenade.

(c) Nous … aux échecs après les cours.

(d) Nous allons … au rugby demain.

(e) Ton prof adore … du ski.

2 To go further, give the right part for each verb as it is used in the sentence.

3 If you have time to spare, translate the complete sentences into English.

Exercice 10.8

Translate these expressions into French. For this exercise, you need two verbs together, and the second one is infinitive, for example:

j'aime jouer   **I like to play**

Some reminders have been put in for you.

1 She likes to play.   aimer, jouer

2 Pauline loves to swim.   adorer, nager/se baigner *

3 Do you want to go for a walk?   vouloir, faire, promenade (f.)

4 We're going to go cycling.   aller, faire, vélo (m.)

5 They (m.) don't like to play tennis.

* There is a slight difference between the two verbs for swimming:

nager   to swim (the action)

but

se baigner   to go for a swim

■ Pauline aime nager

Exercice 10.9

Write these sentences in French, but in the futur proche. Here's the verb aller (to go, to be going) again in full:

aller: to go	
je vais	nous allons
tu vas	vous allez
il va	ils vont
elle va	elles vont

For example:

In the sentence On fait la vaisselle, **we need to change** on fait (we do) **to make it say 'we are going to do', so that** on fait **becomes** on va faire: On va faire la vaisselle

1 Je joue au football.

2 Nous faisons une promenade.

3 Vous jouez au rugby?

4 Elles font du vélo.

5 On joue au tennis.

Exam style   Exercice 10.10

Level 2

Translate these sentences into French.

1 We are going to the cinema tomorrow.   aller, cinéma, demain

2 Do you want to go cycling with me?   vouloir, faire du vélo

3 My parents are going to go for a walk after lunch.   faire une promenade, déjeuner (m.)

4 My friends are going to play tennis at Michel's house.   jouer, chez*

5 I am not going to play football today.   jouer, aujourd'hui

* chez   at the house of; to the house of, for example:

chez Michel   **at/to Michel's house.**

Exam style   Exercice 10.11

Mes loisirs – My leisure activities

Prepare a 30-second presentation on your hobbies.

Work in pairs. Try to speak in French for 30 seconds on your favourite activities. Here are a few points to help you:

Speak about ...

● what your favourite activities are (e.g. cycling, music, sport)

- where you go to do these activities
- who you do them with.

Your partner could then ask questions about (for example):

- how long you have been doing the activities
- how often/when you do them.

Your partner will then make a similar presentation about their own favourite activities.

What you should now know about verb tenses

You have now studied le présent (the present tense) and le futur proche (the future tense with aller). You began by learning about the way verbs work, by looking at several regular -ER (first-group) verbs, as well as the most used irregular ones.

You learned that the present tense is said in two different ways in English (e.g. 'I speak' and 'I am speaking') but only one in French (je parle).

You also recently studied regular -IR (second-group) verbs.

You learned that the word 'infinitive' means the 'name' of a verb.

Finally, you saw how we make the futur proche by adding aller to any infinitive, for example:

elle va réussir   she is going to succeed

Now we can complete the picture.

Les verbes du troisième groupe – Third-group verbs (-RE)

61

The verbs in this group follow the pattern shown below in vendre. The endings are shown in bold, but note that there is no ending after the d in the third person singular.

vendre: to sell	
je vend**s**	nous vend**ons**
tu vend**s**	nous vend**ez**
il vend	ils vend**ent**
elle vend	elles vend**ent**

Exercice 10.12

Write out **one** of the following verbs in full.

1 rendre   to give back, to hand in (for example homework)

2 descendre   to go down(stairs)

3 attendre   to wait (for)

4 entendre   to hear

5 vendre   to sell

6 répondre   to answer

Exam style   Exercice 10.13

Level 1

Give the correct version of each verb for its sentence. If you finish early, try translating the sentences into English.

1 On n'(attendre) pas le bus ici.

2 Tu (entendre)? Il est dix heures.

3 Elle (descendre) à la cuisine.

4 Monsieur Barreau (vendre) sa voiture.

5 Tu ne (rendre) pas ton cahier?

Exam style   Exercice 10.14

Level 2

Translate into French.

1 I hand in my exercise book after lunch.   rendre, cahier (*m.*), déjeuner (*m.*)

2 We go downstairs at 8.00 a.m.   descendre

3 Mum waits for Philippe at our house.   attendre, chez

4 Sophie and Claire do not hear the car.   entendre, voiture (*f.*)

5 Are you selling the house, papa?   vendre, maison (*f.*)

Exercice 10.15

Try rewriting these sentences as questions.

Reminder: To make questions, we can either use est-ce que … or inversion, for example, vous mangez becomes:

Est-ce que vous mangez?

Mangez-vous?

1 Tu peux jouer aux échecs avec Paul.

2 Vous voulez voir un film ce soir à la télé.

3 Simone va au théâtre samedi soir.

4 Tu fais du cyclisme après les cours.

5 On peut jouer au rugby à l'école.

Exam style Exercice 10.16

Listen to and read this conversation and the passage below, then have a go at the questions that follow.

Philippe.	Alors, tu finis tes devoirs cet après-midi, c'est ça?
Marcel.	Oui. Après ça, je vais chez Henri.
Philippe.	Impeccable! Tu as toujours mon bouquin*?
Marcel.	Ben … Oui! Je vais rendre ton bouquin cet après-midi!
Philippe.	Alors, tu vas finir quand, Marcel?
Marcel.	Je ne sais pas.
Henri.	Moi, je vais jouer au foot.
Philippe.	Bon, d'accord.

* le bouquin   a conversational word meaning 'book'

Marcel fait ses devoirs, mais Philippe veut jouer au football chez Henri. Philippe va chez son ami. Il arrive vers deux heures de l'après-midi. Plus tard, à 15 heures, Marcel finit ses devoirs, donc il va chez Henri et les trois copains cherchent des vidéos d'un groupe qui s'appelle Banango. Plus tard, ils sortent dans le jardin d'Henri où ils jouent au foot. Marcel marque un but. Philippe aime écouter de la musique, mais il préfère jouer au football. Henri aussi.

c'est ça?	is that right?	vers deux heures	at about two o'clock
impeccable	brilliant, excellent	plus tard	later
tu as toujours …	(do) you still have …	marquer un but	to score a goal
vers	towards		

Write these sentences in full, completing each one with the correct word from the brackets.

1 … doit finir ses devoirs. (Philippe/Marcel/Henri)

2 Philippe arrive chez Henri … Marcel. (avant/après/avec)

3 Marcel a le … de Philippe. (crayon/ballon/livre)

4 Banango est le nom … (d'un groupe/d'un fruit/d'une boisson)

5 Henri et Philippe … le sport à la musique. (promènent/aiment/préfèrent)

Exam style | Exercice 10.17

Level 1

Write one short sentence for each of these pictures, saying what you and other people are going to do in the holidays.

For example, for a picture of a person swimming, you could write:

En vacances, je vais nager dans la mer.

Each of the five people you mention should be different, for example yourself, your parent, your brother or sister, your friend and so on.

Exam style | Exercice 10.18

Level 2

Compose an email of 80 to 120 words to a friend, saying what you and your family or friends are **going to** do on holiday. You must mention at least **four** of the following:

- où tu vas aller et quand — where you are going and when
- le temps qu'il fait — the weather (where you are going)
- avec qui tu vas voyager — who you are travelling with
- comment tu vas voyager — your method of transport
- trois activités — three activities.

11 Les quatre saisons

In this chapter, you will learn how to speak and write about the four seasons of the year and begin to use more words and expressions to do with hobbies.

Au printemps, Martine aime promener le chien.

■ le printemps

En été, Xavier, Jean et Philippe aiment aller à la plage.

■ l'été

En automne, Christophe et Henri jouent aux boules dans le village.

■ l'automne

En hiver, Florence et Amélie font du ski dans les Alpes.

■ l'hiver

Exercice 11.1

Listen to the audio track, look at the vocabulary and do the exercise that follows. **63**

le printemps	spring	en automne	in autumn
au printemps	in spring	l'hiver (*m.*)	winter
l'été (*m.*)	summer	en hiver	in winter
en été	in summer	il fait beau	it's nice weather
l'automne (*m.*)	autumn	l'escalade (*f.*)	(rock) climbing

Answer the questions in English.

1 What does Georges say he likes to do in springtime?

2 What does Martine think of that?

3 What does Martine like to do at this time of year?

4 What is Georges' reaction?

Exam style Exercice 11.2

64

Listen to the audio track, then, referring to Exercice 11.1 and this one, copy and complete the sentences. Use the verbs in the box; one verb is not needed.

la saison	the season	se bronzer/bronzer	to sunbathe
à la plage	to the beach; at the beach	se baigner	to go for a swim; to bathe
aller en vacances	to go on holiday	faire de la planche à voile	to go windsurfing

aime	préfère	joue
chantez	va	aiment

1 Au printemps, Georges et Martine ... promener le chien.

2 En été, Claire ... se baigner à la plage.

3 Georges adore l'été, parce qu'on ... en vacances.

4 Au printemps, Georges ... au rugby avec ses copains.

5 Jean-Pierre ... faire de la planche à voile.

◯ Les saisons et le temps – Seasons and weather

1 Les quatre saisons:

The seasons have their own special phrases in French. Notice first of all how to say 'in' followed by a season:

en été   en automne   en hiver   but: au printemps (because printemps does not begin with a vowel or silent 'h')

2 Quel temps fait-il?

The weather is quite easy to talk about in French. Here, we will learn how to describe it in the present tense, saying what the weather is like *now*, *often* or *usually*.

Weather expressions with faire

The verb most often used in weather expressions is faire. So, when we ask what the weather is like, we say: Quel temps fait-il?

Incidentally, you have come across the word quel ('which ...?') spelled two different ways. Quel is followed by masculine nouns, quelle by feminine ones. They both add an -s in the plural:

quel garçon (*m.*)? quelle fille (*f.*)? quels garçons (*m.pl.*)? quelles filles (*f.pl.*)?

il fait beau	it's fine	il fait bon	it's pleasant, warm
il fait mauvais	it's bad weather	il fait frais	it's chilly
il fait chaud	it's hot	il fait 27° (degrés)	it's 27°
il fait froid	it's cold		

Using other verbs

il pleut	it rains; it's raining	il gèle	it freezes; it's freezing
il neige	it snows; it's snowing	le soleil brille	the sun shines; the sun is shining

Using il y a

il y a du soleil	it's sunny	il y a des éclairs	there is lightning
il y a du vent	it's windy	il y a des nuages	it's cloudy
il y a du brouillard	it's foggy		

A few weather adjectives

couvert/e	overcast; grey	merveilleux/merveilleuse	wonderful
glacial/e	icy	affreux/affreuse	awful
ensoleillé/e	sunny	agréable	pleasant
nuageux/nuageuse	cloudy	désagréable	unpleasant

Adding more detail

ne ... pas	Il ne fait pas chaud.	It **isn't** hot.
très	Il fait très froid.	It's **very** cold.
trop	Il fait trop froid.	It's **too** cold.
assez	Il fait assez chaud.	It's **quite** hot.
mais	Il fait froid, mais il y a du soleil.	It's cold, **but** it's sunny.
souvent	Il ne neige pas souvent.	It does not snow **often**.
quelquefois	Il fait quelquefois mauvais.	The weather is **sometimes** bad.
maintenant	Il pleut maintenant.	It's raining **now**.
d'habitude	D'habitude il fait beau.	**Usually** it's fine.

À toi – Your turn

Look at the weather on the map. Can you finish these sentences?

(a) Dans le nord il fait …
(b) Dans le sud il y a …
(c) Dans l'est le ciel* est …
(d) Dans l'ouest il …

* le ciel = the sky

Exam style **Exercice 11.3**

Quel temps fait-il?

Give the right French weather expression for each picture, as in the example:

1 Il fait très froid.

1

2

3

4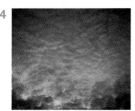

5

6

7

8

9

10

Saying à and en with seasons, months, etc.

You have already learnt about seasons, months and days, but this section is included here so that you can see everything in one place. Study and learn these examples.

Months, seasons and days

in January	**en** janvier*		**in** winter	**en** hiver
in spring	**au** printemps		**on** Tuesday	mardi
in summer	**en** été		**on** Tuesdays	**le** mardi
in autumn	**en** automne			

Countries

in Scotland	en Écosse (*f.*)
in Wales	au Pays de Galles (*m.*)
in the USA	aux États-Unis (*pl.*)

Towns

in Marseilles	à Marseille

* or au mois de ('in the month of'), for example:

au mois de janvier	in the month of January

Exercice 11.4

Vrai ou faux?   True or false?

Answer these questions with Vrai ('true') or Faux ('false'). For those that are false, write a sentence in French to correct the statement.

1 En Afrique, il fait chaud.

2 Il ne pleut pas à Manchester.

3 À Cardiff, il fait 30° en décembre.

4 Il neige à la montagne.

5 En France, en été, il fait chaud.

6 Au printemps, les fleurs poussent*.

7 Dans le désert, il pleut beaucoup.

8 En hiver, il fait chaud en Écosse.

9 Il pleut en Angleterre.

10 Il ne neige pas souvent en Suisse.

* pousser = to grow (as well as 'to push')

Exam style Exercice 11.5

Level 1

Rewrite these sentences, inserting the word that would make the best sense.

1 Il … chaud et beau. (fait, faire, froid)

2 Il y a du … (salle, salon, soleil)

3 En Angleterre, il fait quelquefois … . (bleu, beau, boisson)

4 Il pleut, mais il fait … chaud. (assez, assis, asseyez)

5 Il fait très froid … (argent, arbre, aujourd'hui)

Exam style Exercice 11.6

Level 2

Translate these sentences into French. Key word reminders are provided.

1 It is sunny today, but it is cold. faire, beau, aujourd'hui, froid

2 In the summer, it is warm. été (*m.*), chaud

3 In the autumn, it is fine, but it is not hot. automne (*m.*)

4 In winter, it snows and it is cold. hiver (*m.*), neiger

5 It does not often snow in Africa. souvent, Afrique (*f.*)

6 It is not very hot. faire, chaud

7 In France, it snows sometimes. quelquefois

8 Sometimes, it is quite hot. faire, assez

9 It is cold today. faire

10 In spring, it is quite cold. printemps (*m.*)

Exercice 11.7

65

Read and listen to the passage, then do the exercise.

Magali va à l'hypermarché le vendredi. Il y a un marché dans son village deux fois par semaine, le vendredi et le samedi. Pourtant, il y a un plus grand choix de produits à l'hyper. Magali habite en France depuis dix ans, mais elle est d'origine sénégalaise. Au Sénégal, on parle français. Au Sénégal, la famille de Magali habite dans la capitale, Dakar.

In the paragraph above, find the French equivalent of the following phrases.

1 on Fridays

2 twice a week

3 the hypermarket

4 however

5 a greater choice

6 of Senegalese origin

7 in Senegal, French is spoken

Depuis – Since

What do you think Magali habite en France depuis dix ans means?

In English, we would say 'Magali has been living in France for ten years', but in French we say that she 'is living in France since ten years'. We use the present tense because she still is living there.

Les verbes: lire

Un verbe irrégulier

lire: to read	
je lis	nous lisons
tu lis	vous lisez
il lit	ils lisent
elle lit	elles lisent

■ Quand il pleut, je lis un roman.

■ Je lis

Exam style Exercice 11.8

Il ne pleut pas souvent en France en été. Quelquefois il neige en hiver, mais d'habitude il fait beau et assez froid. À Charleville, il y a une patinoire et deux cinémas, mais il n'y a pas de piscine. La patinoire est ouverte le lundi et le jeudi, sauf en été. En été, elle est fermée. Au mois de juillet je vais venir en Angleterre: je vais passer 12 jours à Bristol, du 4 au 16. D'habitude on va en Italie, mais cette année c'est différent! Maman veut essayer du rosbif dans un restaurant et papa veut boire de la bière anglaise!

venir (*irreg.*)	to come
rester	to stay
essayer	to try
cette année	this year
prendre (*irreg.*)	to take; to have (food, drink or a meal)
boire (*irreg.*)	to drink
le rosbif	roast beef (also a French nickname for an Englishman!)
la bière	the beer
sauf	except

Using the information above, write an email in French of 80 to 120 words. Say that:

- it rains often in England but it is sunny sometimes
- in [your town], there is a cinema and a swimming pool
- the cinema is always open, except on Thursdays
- you (je, of course!) are going to France in the summer
- you are going to be in Avignon from 8 to 25 August.

Les verbes: prendre and boire

These two irregular verbs are essential for talking about food and drink: prendre means 'to take', but is also used for eating. Boire means 'to drink'.

prendre: to take; to have a meal	
je prends	nous prenons
tu prends	vous prenez
il prend	ils prennent
elle prend	elles prennent

boire: to drink	
je bois	nous buvons
tu bois	vous buvez
il boit	ils boivent
elle boit	elles boivent

Exam style Exercice 11.9

Give the right verb form for each one of the verbs in brackets.

1 Tu … un coca? (prend, prends, prenons)

2 Non, je … du café. (boivent, boit, bois)

3 Nous … beaucoup d'eau. (buvez, buvons, boit)

4 Ils … le petit-déjeuner au café. (prennent, prenons, prenez)

5 Elle … de la limonade. (boivent, bois, boit)

Exam style | Exercice 11.10

Level 2

Translate into French.

1 I have some orange juice.   prendre, jus (*m.*) d'orange

2 They drink tea in England.   thé (*m.*)

3 They (*f.*) drink hot chocolate.   chocolat (*m.*)

4 Do you (*pl.*) take sugar?   sucre (*m.*)

5 Martin drinks strawberry cordial.   sirop (*m.*), fraise (*f.*)

Demonstratives

Level 2

How to say 'this', 'that', 'these', 'those' before nouns

this/that				these/those		
m.	ce	ce garçon	this boy/that boy	ces	ces garçons	these boys/those boys
m. before vowel or silent 'h'	cet	cet homme	this man/that man	ces	ces hommes	these men/those men
f.	cette	cette fille	this girl/that girl	ces	ces filles	these girls/those girls

For example:

cette année   this year *or* that year

In the singular, all these French words can mean either 'this' or 'that'.

The plural word means either 'these' or 'those'.

> Reminder: ce garçon can mean 'this boy' *or* 'that boy'; ces filles can mean 'these girls' *or* 'those girls' and so on.

Exercice 11.11

Level 2

Write these nouns with the right demonstrative (ce, cet, cette or ces), as in the example:

le garçon – ce garçon

1	le crayon	8	les chaises	15	la gomme
2	la carte	9	la table	16	la chambre
3	le livre	10	le prof	17	la cuisine
4	la fenêtre	11	l'ami	18	les pièces
5	les portes	12	les cahiers	19	les jardins
6	la règle	13	l'enfant	20	le beurre
7	le tableau	14	le stylo		

Exam style Exercice 11.12

66

Listen to the audio track, look at the vocabulary, then do the exercise that follows.

oublier	to forget
bête	silly
comme	like (e.g. she's like you)
en vacances	on holiday
les Landes	Landes (part of south-western France)
quinze jours	a fortnight
le Sénégal	Senegal (a French speaking country in western Africa)
louer	to rent; to hire
appareil photo (*m.*)	camera

Answer the questions in English.

1 What has Chloé forgotten (about Claire)?

2 When is Magali's birthday?

3 What's the weather like at the time of Jean-Pierre's birthday?

4 Where do Jean-Pierre and Claire usually go for the summer holidays?

5 Where are they going this year?

6 What does Claire say they are going to do?

7 What does Claire tell Chloé not to forget?

Exam style Exercice 11.13

Join the sentence halves, so that the sentences make sense.

1 Chloé oublie

2 Au Sénégal on

3 Claire et Jean-Pierre

4 En été il

5 Le premier août

(a) mange du couscous.

(b) est en été.

(c) fait beau et chaud.

(d) la date de l'anniversaire de Claire.

(e) vont se baigner.

Exam style Exercice 11.14

Level 2

Translate these sentences into French.

1 Claire forgets her camera. oublier, appareil photo (*m.*)

2 Chloé does not forget her father's birthday. anniversaire (*m.*), père (*m.*)

111

3 Chloé and Magali are going to Bandol.   aller

4 We (*on*) usually go to England.   d'habitude, Angleterre (*f.*)

5 I am not going to Tunisia this year.   Tunisie (*f.*), année (*f.*)

Les verbes: partir

Partir is an important verb, partly because several other useful verbs follow the same pattern. You have met two of them already.

partir: to leave, to set off, to go away	
je **pars**	nous **partons**
tu **pars**	vous **partez**
il **part**	ils **partent**
elle **part**	elles **partent**

Other verbs like partir:

sortir   to go out   dormir   to sleep

sentir   to feel   mentir   to (tell a) lie

servir   to serve

This means that sortir, dormir, servir, sentir and mentir all have a three-letter stem in the singular and a four-letter stem in the plural:

tu **mens**   il **dort**   elles **serv**ent   nous **sort**ons

This can be quite a good short cut to remembering how they are spelled, since all their endings follow the same pattern and you only need to learn those once!

Exercice 11.15

Here are two short conversations, to practise dormir, mentir, sortir and partir.

Practise them and be prepared to use them.

Des ami(e)s sont en vacances, au camping. Il est 23 h!

Petit dialogue 1

A.   Hé! Tu dors?

B.   Oui. Je dors. Et toi?

A.   Non! Je ne dors pas. Et toi, tu ne dors pas! Tu mens!

B.   Oui je mens!

A.   Alors je sors.

Petit dialogue 2

C.	Hé! Vous dormez?
D, E.	Oui! Nous dormons!
C.	Mais vous mentez! Vous ne dormez pas!
D, E.	Non! Nous ne dormons pas. Nous partons.
C.	Vous partez?
F.	Qu'est-ce qu'ils font?
G.	Ils partent …
F.	Alors moi, je dors.

Exercice 11.16

Anne-Marie receives an email from Joselle, her friend who lives in Switzerland.

De: joselle@…

À: ambenoit@ …

Objet: Bonjour

Bonjour Anne-Marie,

Je suis ravie de recevoir ton dernier e-mail. Alors, c'est bientôt les vacances! J'adore les vacances. D'habitude, nous allons en Italie ou en Grèce, parce que mes parents adorent le soleil et parce qu'ils s'intéressent beaucoup à l'histoire. C'est assez amusant, mais ma sœur et moi, on veut visiter la capitale de la France! Alors cette année on va aller à Paris! On va louer un appartement près de la rivière! On ne va pas visiter les palais et les musées; on va faire du shopping dans les grands magasins et on va manger dans des restaurants. C'est génial, n'est-ce pas? Écris-moi vite et raconte-moi tes projets de vacances!

Amitiés, Joselle

In Joselle's email, find the French equivalent of the following phrases.

1 I am delighted to

2 They're very interested in history

3 It's quite fun

4 We want to visit the capital

5 We're going to go to Paris

6 We're going to rent

7 Near the river

8 It's brilliant, isn't it?

9 Write soon

10 Your holiday plans

Exercice 11.17

Referring back to Exercice 11.16, answer these questions in English.

1 Where does her family normally go on holiday?

2 Why do they go there? (Give two reasons.)

3 Give two details about where they will be staying in Paris.

4 Give two things Joselle says they will be doing and one thing they will *not*.

Exam style | Exercice 11.18

Level 2

Role play

A's friend B phones to discuss the holidays. Take it in turns to be A and B.

A.

Hello. How are you?

I'm fine. It's the holidays soon.

We're going to the Vercors*.

[Give two activities*] What about you?

What are you going to do?

When are you going to come home**?

B.

Ça va. Et toi?

Oui! Tu vas partir?

Cool! Qu'est-ce que tu vas faire?

Nous, on va faire du camping.

Des randonnées, du vélo …

Euh … fin juillet, je pense.

* The Massif du Vercors is a hilly region in southern France where all sorts of outdoor activities can be tried (see below).

** For 'to come home', use the verb rentrer.

la randonnée	hiking	le canoë-kayak	kayaking
l'alpinisme (*m.*)	mountaineering	la spéléologie (*f.*)	caving
l'aviron (*m.*)	rowing		

Exam style | Exercice 11.19

Level 2

Now write, in French, an answer to Joselle's email from Exercice 11.16, as if you were her correspondant. Write 80 to 120 words about at least four of the following:

- tes projets de vacances — your holiday plans
- le temps qu'il fait (la météo) — the weather
- une visite que tu vas faire — somewhere you plan to visit
- ce que tu aimes faire en vacances — what you like to do on holiday
- quelque chose que tu veux acheter — something you want to buy.

Après les vacances

In this chapter, you will learn all about a whole range of expressions using avoir and more words and expressions to do with leisure activities and travel.

■ J'ai faim!

■ J'ai froid!

■ J'ai chaud!

■ J'ai soif!

Idioms with avoir

When we talk of an idiom in language learning, we mean a phrase that, while expressing the same idea as a phrase in another language, uses completely different words.

For example the English phrase 'I have been learning French *for* five years' becomes 'I am learning French *since* five years' when you say the same thing in French.

Many expressions that use avoir in French do not use the verb 'to have' in English. Much earlier we met:

J'ai huit ans   I **am** eight years old

There will be more examples of avoir idioms as we progress. For now, here are a few to start you off:

avoir faim	to be hungry	avoir peur	to be afraid
avoir soif	to be thirsty	avoir raison	to be right
avoir chaud	to be hot	avoir tort	to be wrong
avoir froid	to be cold	avoir mal	to be in pain

Exercice 12.1

Here are all the parts of avoir froid (to be cold). Give the English for each one. The first two are done for you.

j'ai froid	I am cold	nous avons froid
tu as froid	you (*sing.*) are cold	vous avez froid
il a froid		ils ont froid
elle a froid		elles ont froid
on a froid		

Exercice 12.2

Give the French equivalent for the following phrases.

1   She is cold.
2   We are hungry.
3   I am thirsty.
4   You (*sing.*) are hot.
5   They (*m.*) are hungry.

6   He is right.
7   You (*pl.*) are thirsty.
8   We (nous) are wrong.
9   They (*f.*) are thirsty.
10 We (on) are in pain.

Idioms with avoir in the negative

To say 'I am not hungry', 'she isn't cold' and so on, make the avoir part negative, then add faim, soif, chaud or froid last:

je n'ai pas faim, elle n'a pas froid and so on.

Exercice 12.3

Write these expressions in the negative, then give the English for your *answers*.
The first is done for you.

1 J'ai faim.   Je n'ai pas faim   I'm not hungry

2 Tu as soif.

3 Il a peur.

4 Elle a froid.

5 Nous avons soif.

6 Vous avez mal.

7 Tu as chaud.

8 Ils ont froid.

9 Vous avez faim.

10 Elles ont tort.

Exercice 12.4

67

Listen to the audio track, then give the words missing from the text below. You
will find them after the text. One of them is not needed.

Magali est dans le [1] devant la maison. Elle parle à la [2], Madame Demailly.

Mme Demailly.	Bonjour, Magali! Ça va?
Magali.	Bonjour, Madame Demailly. Ça va bien, merci, et vous?
Mme Demailly.	Ça va bien, merci. Déjà rentrée de vacances?
Magali.	Oui. Il fait beau aujourd'hui. Qu'est-ce que vous faites?
Mme Demailly.	Je [3] dans le jardin. Mais toi, tu es très bronzée! Il fait chaud au Sénégal?
Magali.	Ah oui. Le soleil [4] tous les jours au Sénégal!
Mme Demailly.	Bien sûr. Et qu'est-ce qu'on fait, en été, là-bas?
Magali.	Bien moi, je bronze tous les jours à la plage et quand il fait trop chaud, je me baigne dans la mer. J'aime aussi faire de la planche à [5]
Mme Demailly.	Formidable! Moi, je fais du camping. Ma fille grimpe aux arbres! Puis nous faisons des pique-niques et des promenades en forêt.

voile	jardin	travaille
brille	voisine	foot

le voisin/la voisine	the neighbour (*m./f.*)
déjà rentrée de vacances?	already back from holiday?
bronzer	to sunbathe
briller	to shine
tous les jours	every day
qu'est-ce qu'on fait?	what do people do?
se baigner	to go for a swim
faire de la planche à voile	to go windsurfing
faire un pique-nique	to have a picnic
la plage	the beach
grimper	to climb

Exercice 12.5

Give the right part of avoir for each gap.

1 Magali … six semaines de vacances.

2 Elle … beaucoup d'amis.

3 Martine … un livre de bandes dessinées.

4 Mme Demailly et Magali … chaud.

5 Les parents de Magali … froid quand il y a du vent.

6 J'… très faim.

7 Vous … des baguettes?

8 Oui, nous … un grand choix de pains.

9 Martine … soif quand elle joue au tennis?

10 Non, elle … sa bouteille d'eau.

Time to spare? Choose five of your answers and say what they mean in English.

Exam style | Exercice 12.6

Samedi matin

Read the sentences below, then answer the questions.

Magali parle à Mme Demailly. Elles discutent pendant que Marie-Claire écoute la radio.

Dans la cuisine, maman chante. Papa et Chloé sont à Paris parce que Chloé veut visiter une galerie d'art. Moi, je fais mes devoirs et je regarde la télévision. Philippe et Nicole, les autres voisins de Magali, vont à la pêche dans l'étang du village.

1 Who is Magali speaking to?

2 What is Marie-Claire doing while they chat?

3 What is maman doing in the kitchen?

4 Who are Philippe and Nicole?

5 What are Philippe and Nicole doing?

Exam style | Exercice 12.7

Work in pairs. Look back to Exercice 12.4 to see the conversation between Magali and Madame Demailly.

First, work through the dialogue, each taking a part.

Then change the details to suit your own choices, like the country you go to, the weather and the activities you prefer on holiday.

Exam style | Exercice 12.8

Listen to the audio track and answer the questions in English.

68

le camping	the campsite	chatter*	to chat (online)
le paysage	the landscape	une boîte	a box
tout autour	all around	en argent	(made) of silver
par terre	on the ground	ouah!	wow!

* The ch at the beginning of chatter is pronounced like the English word it comes from. It only means to chat online, not face-to-face, which is bavarder.

1 What does Magali do on holiday apart from windsurfing and swimming?

2 Who plays tennis?

3 What does her sister Chloé do?

4 What does Mme Demailly think about what Chloé does?

5 Where does Mme Demailly find the box?

Now try to remember as many expressions as you can from Exercices 12.7 and 12.8 that include first-group -ER verbs.

An 'expression' here means **subject and verb**, for example Mme Demailly trouve.

69

Read as you listen to the passage, then do the exercise.

Magali passe les grandes vacances avec toute sa famille sur la côte sénégalaise, pas loin de Dakar, où habitent ses oncles et tantes, ses cousins et cousines et ses grands-parents. Le Sénégal se trouve en Afrique de l'Ouest, face à l'Atlantique. À Dakar, la capitale, on peut faire de la voile et beaucoup d'autres sports nautiques. Il y a des yachts amarrés au port, avec les bateaux de pêche.

Après les grandes vacances, Magali parle à la voisine, Mme Demailly. Elle demande à Magali: «Qu'est-ce qu'on fait en été au Sénégal?». Magali fait beaucoup de choses. Elle fait de la planche à voile, elle nage dans la mer, elle joue au foot sur la plage avec ses cousins et elle dessine.

Magali dessine bien. Sa sœur Chloé ne quitte pas sa tablette. Elle passe beaucoup de temps à chatter avec ses amies en ligne. Soudain, Mme Demailly voit une petite boîte en argent par terre. Elle est très vieille et très sale. Elle est noire! Magali regarde la boîte.

les grandes vacances (*f.pl.*)	the summer holidays	bien	well
amarrés	moored	soudain	suddenly
un port	a harbour	voir	to see
une tablette	a tablet	sale	dirty

1 Read the passage out loud to practise your French accent. Your teacher will play the audio, in small chunks if necessary, before you try to repeat the story. You can compare your accent with the audio.

2 Select the correct answer from the options.

(a) Dakar is … (on the coast/inland/in the mountains)

(b) Senegal is in western … (Europe/Asia/Africa)

(c) The little box looks to be made of … (gold/copper/silver)

Exercice 12.10

Unscramble these words from Magali's holiday.

1 ANGE

2 OLIVE

3 ERM

4 SCAAVCNE

5 NSEDSIE

6 SOOSPIN

7 TOBIE

8 RAGNET

9 TORP

10 TELETBAT

13 La boîte en argent

In this chapter, we shall be following the story of the silver box, and talking and writing about visiting cafés and restaurants. There are several new verbs introduced in this chapter: they are set out here for when you do the corresponding exercises, though you will also find them in the reference section at the back of the book.

Exercice 13.1

70

La boîte en argent – The Silver Box (1)

Study the vocabulary before listening to the audio, then answer the questions.

qu'est-ce que tu vois?	what do you see?
attendez!	wait!; hang on!
nettoyer	to clean
un produit	a (cleaning) product
montrez-moi!	show me!
qui est-ce?	who is it?
je sais	I know (a fact)
tu connais	you (s.) know (a person or place)
qu'est-ce qu'on va faire?	what are we going to do?
savoir (*irreg.*)	to know (facts)
connaître (*irreg.*)	to know (people and places)
il faut (+ *infin.*)	it is necessary to ...
réfléchir	to think (carefully)
peut-être	perhaps
ouvrir (*irreg.*)	to open
découvrir (*irreg.* like ouvrir)	to discover
à suivre	to be continued

Select the correct missing words to fill the gaps.

1 The box is ... (old/new/oval)

2 On the lid there are ... (designs/initials/numbers)

3 ... cleans the box. (Mme Demailly/Chloé/Magali)

4 Magali's friend is ... (Jean-Pierre/Jean-Patrick/Jean-Philippe)

◯ L'alphabet français – The French alphabet

Learning the alphabet in French is essential. From now on, look for opportunities to practise spelling in French, until you can do it easily.

Exercice 13.2

71

Listen to the audio and repeat these groups of letters.

ABCD ~ EFGH ~ IJ ~ KLMN ~ OPQR ~ STUV ~ WXYZ

Exercice 13.3

72

Work in pairs, then groups of three, asking how to spell people's names and other objects, for example:

1 – Comment ça s'appelle?

   – Ça s'appelle un «violon».

   – Comment écrit-on «violon»?

   – V I O L O N.

2 – Elle s'appelle comment?

   – Elle s'appelle Julie.

   – Comment ça s'écrit?

   – Ça s'écrit J U L I E.

3 – Qu'est-ce que c'est?

   – C'est de la brioche.

   – Ça s'écrit comment?

   – Ça s'écrit B R I O C H E.

4 – Comment tu t'appelles?

   – Thierry.

   – Comment ça s'écrit?

   – Ça s'écrit T H I E R R Y.

épeler	to spell
comment ça s'écrit?	how do you spell it?
ça s'écrit comment?	how do you spell it?
comment écrit-on ...?	how do you spell ...?
la brioche	the brioche (a cake-like loaf)
comment ça s'appelle?	what is that called?
le violon	the violin

◯ Les verbes: savoir and connaître

Two verbs, both meaning 'to know', but with important differences!

savoir: to know (a fact); to know how to ...*	
je sais	nous savons
tu sais	vous savez
il sait	ils savent
elle sait	elles savent

* Savoir followed by an infinitive also means 'to know *how to ...*' and you don't need to translate 'how to', for example:

Georges sait nager.   Georges knows how to swim.

connaître: to know (a person or place)	
je connais	nous connaissons
tu connais	vous connaissez
il connaît	ils connaissent
elle connaît	elles connaissent

Reminder: The accent circonflexe (il, elle connaît) makes no difference to the sound of the word.

Exam style | Exercice 13.4

Checking above, complete each sentence with the correct verb part, for example:

Papa ... chanter. (savoir) – Papa sait chanter.

1   Georges ... ouvrir la boîte. (savoir)

2   M. Simmoneau ... la maison. (connaître)

3   Vous ... nager? (savoir)

4   Non, je ne ... pas nager. (savoir)

5   Martine ... mon ami Jules. (connaître)

6   Nous ... écrire en français. (savoir)

7   ...-tu lire en anglais? (savoir)

8   On ... les chants de Noël. (connaître)

9   Philippe et Marcel ... faire du VTT. (savoir)

10 ...-vous la famille Durand? (connaître)

Les verbes: ouvrir

This verb is a real cuckoo in the nest – an -IR verb that thinks it's an -ER verb (it has the same endings)!

Not only important itself, ouvrir serves as a model for several other verbs.*

ouvrir: to open	
j'ouvre	nous ouvrons
tu ouvres	vous ouvrez
il ouvre	ils ouvrent
elle ouvre	elles ouvrent

* Here are some other 'cuckoo' verbs like ouvrir!

couvrir	to cover	souffrir	to suffer
découvrir	to discover	offrir	to offer; to give (a gift)

Les verbes: suivre

You may have noticed à suivre ('to be continued').

Here is the whole verb:

suivre: to follow	
je suis*	nous suivons
tu suis	vous suivez
il suit	ils suivent
elle suit	elles suivent

* It is easy to muddle up je suis meaning 'I follow' with je suis meaning 'I am', but just look at what would make better sense:

je suis ma mère   *I am* my mother or *I'm following* my mother?

Exam style Exercice 13.5

Checking above, complete each sentence with the correct verb part. The exercise includes other verbs that you have already learned.

1   Georges ... la fenêtre de la cuisine. (ouvrir)

2   Marie-Claire ... la porte du salon. (fermer)

3   Pourquoi n'...-tu pas la fenêtre? (ouvrir)

4   Parce qu'il ... froid. (faire)

5   ...-il son livre? (finir)

6   Non, il ... en ce moment. (lire)

7   Est-ce qu'il ... sa trousse? (ouvrir)

8   On ne ... pas. (savoir)

9   Ils ... le magasin à neuf heures. (ouvrir)

10 Vous ... les instructions. (suivre)

Exam style Exercice 13.6

Give a correct pronoun (je, tu, il, elle and so on) for each gap.

Note that, depending on the context, il, elle and on are interchangeable in exercises like this one, since they have the same verb forms. The same is true for ils and elles.

1   ... suit son père à la plage.

2   À Noël, ... ouvrons les cadeaux.

3   ... veux un croissant, chérie?

4   Oui, ... veux bien, papa.

5   ... suit la route de Nîmes.

6   ... ouvrent la boîte.

7   D'habitude, ... suivons les instructions.

8   ... ouvrez à quelle heure, s'il vous plaît?

9   ... veulent entrer dans le café.

10 ... es français ou anglais?

Exercice 13.7

Saying what *does not* happen

Read aloud and then translate these phrases. Some have two possible English versions.

1 Il ne trouve pas

2 Nous n'écoutons pas

3 Vous ne continuez pas

4 On n'écrit pas

5 Tu ne lis pas

Exam style   Exercice 13.8

73

Listen to the audio track, then answer the questions in English.

le temps	the weather (also 'time', so be aware of the context!)
du beau temps	some fine weather
tous les jours	every day
toute la journée	all day
tout de suite	immediately
il fait beau	it is fine (weather)
le déluge	the downpour
en pleine forme	on top form; in good health
il pleut	it rains; it's raining
sec (*m.*), sèche (*f.*)	dry
même	same
payer	to pay for
quelle histoire!	what an embarrassment!/what a fiasco!

1 What is this year's weather like?

2 On what day did it rain heavily?

3 Who take ages to choose their meals in the restaurant?

Exercice 13.9

Write these sentences in the negative.

1 Charles entre dans la bibliothèque.

2 Oncle Jules descend de la voiture.

3 Sophie et Marc arrivent.

4 Ma mère part avant cinq heures.

5 Après le concert, nous sortons tout de suite du théâtre.

Exercice 13.10

Read the following while listening to the audio track.

Papa, maman, Magali et Chloé sont à Dakar au restaurant «Les Trois Fourchettes». Il y a des menus à 3.000, à 4.000 et à 5.000 CFA. Magali et papa regardent le menu à 10.000 et se décident tout de suite, mais Chloé et maman ne sont pas sûres. Papa choisit un thiéboudienne et Magali choisit un steak. Maman décide de prendre le saumon mais Chloé préfère le poulet au couscous.

> Reminder: The local currency in Senegal is Central African Francs (CFA).
> A 10,000 franc menu would cost about 15 euros (2018).

Now simply listen, looking at the vocabulary and answer the questions as soon as you can.

messieurs dames	ladies and gentlemen	le steak-frites	steak and chips
le menu	the fixed-price menu	bien sûr	of course
la carte	the menu of individual dishes	je voudrais	I would like
sûr	sure; certain	changer d'avis	to change one's mind
le thiéboudienne	a Senegalese fish dish	c'est ça?	is that right?
le poulet au couscous	chicken with couscous	enfin, je crois!	well, I think so!
le saumon	salmon		

Who (out of maman, papa, Magali and Chloé) *might* say these things.

1 Moi, ce soir, je mange du poisson.

2 Je mange la même chose que Magali.

3 Mon premier choix, c'est le saumon.

4 J'aime la volaille* mais je préfère la viande rouge.

* volaille (*f.*)   poultry

Exercice 13.11

Listen again to the audio. Can you hear the expressions below? Try jotting them down in French and do not worry about spelling!

1 Are you ready to order?   4 What are you having?

2 I'm going to have ...   5 I would like the chicken.

3 May I have ...?   6 No, wait ...

13 La boîte en argent

14 On mange où?

In this chapter, you will have a chance to practise lots of the French you have learned so far and to learn more about the language of restaurants and cafés.

75

Listen to the audio, study the vocabulary and answer the questions in English.

le lendemain	the next day	déguster	to sample
quand même	nonetheless; anyway	de temps en temps	from time to time
raconter	to tell; to recount (*a story*)	les fruits de mer	seafood
		un bistrot	a small restaurant
raconte!	tell me more!	des moules	mussels
composé de	made up of	arrêter	to stop
embêtant	annoying	arrête!	stop!
d'habitude	usually	tu me donnes faim	you're making me hungry
les pâtes (italiennes)	pasta		

According to what you hear, are these statements true or false?

1 It is cheaper to eat out in Senegal than in France.

2 A visit to a fish restaurant is not ideal for all of Magali's family.

3 Magali and Mme Demailly both like Italian food.

4 Papa wants to try seafood sometimes.

5 The local restaurant serving mussels is big.

Exercice 14.2

Listen again. Pick out the French for:

1 less expensive (moins cher/plus cher/aussi cher)

2 it's a dish (c'est une assiette/c'est un plat/c'est une tasse)

3 everyone (tous les jours/tout le monde/beaucoup de monde)

4 next to the beach (près de la plage/presque la plage/à côté de la plage)

Exercice 14.3

Using Exercice 14.2 to help you, give the French for:

1 less interesting

2 it's a chicken dish (a dish of chicken)

3 everyone likes couscous

4 next to the village

Exercice 14.4

Listen as you read, then do the exercise.

On est au restaurant «Chez Nadia». Tochiko et ses amies entrent dans la salle.

Tochiko.	Chouette! J'adore ce restaurant!
Alice.	Moi aussi. Et puis, manger ici, ce n'est pas cher!
Joséphine.	C'est vrai. Monsieur! On peut s'installer?
Serveur.	Bien sûr! Vous êtes combien?
Joséphine.	On est trois.
Serveur.	Pas de problème! Où vous voulez!
Tochiko.	On se met où?
Alice.	Là. Près de la fenêtre. C'est joli, et on peut tout voir.
Tochiko.	D'accord.
Serveur.	J'apporte la carte, mesdemoiselles!
Tochiko.	Merci, monsieur.

s'installer	to settle in; take a seat	près de	near (to)
on se met où?	where shall we sit?	tout	everything
se mettre	to stand or sit in a certain place (to 'put oneself')	apporter	to bring
		mesdemoiselles	young ladies

Prepare and perform the dialogue above in class.

14 On mange où?

128

Exercice 14.5

77

After listening to the audio, read the text out loud, in small sections, to practise your accent.

«Chez Nadia»

«Chez Nadia», c'est un restaurant algérien. En France, il y a beaucoup de restaurants étrangers. Nadia est une amie de Christine, la mère de Tochiko. C'est Nadia qui fait la cuisine dans son restaurant. Tochiko adore la cuisine algérienne. Vendredi soir, elle va «Chez Nadia» avec ses deux amies Alice et Joséphine. Le serveur apporte la carte. La carte est très bonne et très longue! Tochiko regarde les entrées, les plats principaux et les desserts. Elle ne sait pas quoi choisir! Elle demande à ses amies: «Qu'est-ce vous allez prendre?». Joséphine répond la première:

Je vais prendre le couscous au poulet et aux légumes.

– Moi, je voudrais une salade de riz avec des haricots, dit Alice.

– Tu n'as pas faim? demande Tochiko.

– Si! Mais j'aimerais du couscous après!

– D'accord. Qu'est-ce qu'on va boire?

– De l'eau … et … du coca.

quoi	what
je voudrais	I would like (from the verb vouloir)
j'aimerais	I would like (from the verb aimer)

Exam style Exercice 14.6

Refer back to the text just heard. Answer in English.

1 What sort of place is 'Chez Nadia'?

2 Who does the cooking there?

3 Who is Nadia?

4 When is Tochiko going to 'Chez Nadia'?

5 Who is she going with?

6 What is remarkable about the menu?

7 Why does Tochiko need to ask her friends what they are having?

8 What do they all decide to have to drink?

Exercice 14.7

Design a menu for an Algerian restaurant in France.

> **Reminder:** The background and decoration have to make you think of North Africa and everything written on the menu has to be in French!

To get you started, match up each of the dishes below with the section heading it is supposed to come under. The five section headings are:

1 Nos entrées
2 Nos plats principaux
3 Nos fromages
4 Nos desserts
5 Nos boissons

Coupe spéciale Nadia	'Nadia's special' ice-cream dish
Couscous au poulet et aux légumes	Chicken and vegetable couscous
Salade de riz aux haricots	Rice salad with beans
Eau minérale gazeuse	Fizzy bottled water
Salade de fruits	Fruit salad
Camembert	Camembert
Glaces (une, deux ou trois boules)	Ice cream (one, two or three scoops)
(Fromage de) chèvre	Goat's cheese
Coca Cola®	Coca Cola®
Brochette d'agneau	Lamb kebab
Thé à la menthe	Mint tea
Champignons à l'ail	Mushrooms with garlic
Taboulé	A sort of couscous salad
Sorbet au citron	Lemon sorbet
Omelette au fromage ou aux champignons	Cheese or mushroom omelette
Vin rouge ou blanc en pichet	White or red wine in a carafe

Exercice 14.8

Once again, listen as you read, then perform the following in class:

Mme Demailly parle au père de Magali.

Mme Demailly.   Salut, André! Alors, en vacances, vous découvrez de nouveaux restaurants!

Papa.   C'est vrai. Mais en France on fait des pique-niques à la campagne.

Mme Demailly.   Des pique-niques! Manger en plein air! Profiter de la nature, du soleil, des oiseaux qui chantent dans les arbres …

Papa.   Des moustiques …!

Mme Demailly.   Ah oui! Au fait, qu'est-ce que vous prenez?

Papa.   Ma femme achète du pain, du beurre et du fromage, et les filles vont à la charcuterie.

Mme Demailly.   Et qu'est-ce qu'elles trouvent?

Papa.   Des salades préparées, des carottes râpées, du céleri, des tomates, et bien sûr du jambon, du saucisson et du pâté.

Mme Demailly.   Bravo les filles! Et qu'est-ce que vous aimez boire?

Papa.   De l'eau pour nous et de l'Orangina® pour elles.

à la campagne	in the countryside	la charcuterie	the deli
en plein air	in the open air; outdoors	le céleri	celery
profiter de	to enjoy; to take advantage of	râpé	grated
un oiseau	a bird	la viande	the meat
le moustique	the mosquito	le jambon	the ham

Exam style   Exercice 14.9

Answer the questions in English.

1 What does Mme Demailly think of picnics?

2 What does papa mention that is not so pleasant?

3 Who buys the cheese?

4 Where do Magali and Chloé buy the picnic ingredients?

5 Who has what to drink?

Exercice 14.10

Say which verb each of the words in bold type comes from, for example:

Il remplit le verre – remplir

1 Magali et Chloé **achètent** de la viande.

2 Mme Demailly **parle** au papa de Magali.

3 Chloé **choisit** du céleri*.

4 Ils **vont** à la campagne.

5 Elle **va** à la plage.

* céleri (*m.*)   celery

Exam style | Exercice 14.11

 Level 2

Translate these sentences into French.

1 You (*sing.*) buy three kilos of tomatoes.   un kilo, tomate (*f.*)

2 Marie and Julien go out at 8 p.m.   sortir

3 My mother speaks to the baker in the shop.   boulanger (*m.*)

4 I find my grandmother's cat.   trouver

5 You (*sing.*) do not choose a dress.   robe (*f.*)

Here are some more for early finishers:

6 Marcel does not want to go into the shop.

7 I am reading Marc Levy's latest novel.   dernier, roman (*m.*)

8 We go to Biarritz every year.

9 The dog goes into the house.

10 She does not get out of the car.   descendre (de)

More practice with reflexive ('selfie') verbs

If you need a reminder, look back at Chapter 4!

■ Je me lève à dix heures!

■ Je me repose toute la journée!

Here are some new reflexive verbs to add to the ones you already know:

se trouver	to be situated; to be somewhere (*literally = 'to find oneself'*)
s'arrêter	to stop
se disputer	to argue
se reposer	to rest
se rappeler	to remember

Reflexive verbs in the negative

Simply put **ne** before the reflexive pronoun and **pas** after the verb:

Je me lave I wash myself, I am washing myself

Je ne me lave pas I don't wash myself, I am not washing myself

Stick to this word order and you will not go wrong, for example:

Nous nous trouvons – Nous ne nous trouvons pas

Exam style Exercice 14.12

Translate into French.

1 I stop at the swimming pool.   s'arrêter, piscine (*f.*)

2 She argues with her brother.   se disputer avec

3 We rest after lunch.   se reposer, déjeuner (*m.*)

4 You (*sing.*) find yourself in the town centre. se trouver, centre-ville (*m.*)

5 He argues with me.   avec moi

Here are some more for early finishers:

6 The bus stops in front of the cinema. s'arrêter, cinéma (*m.*)

7 Maman rests before the film. se reposer, film (*m.*)

8 Pierre finds himself at the beach. se trouver

9 Christine's car stops. s'arrêter

10 I get up at 6 a.m. every morning. se lever, matin (*m.*)

Exercice 14.13

These sentences have mistakes, shown in **bold**. Give the right version of each expression.

1 Maman se **levons** ce matin. X

2 Pierre s'**arrêtez** aux feux*. X

3 Je me **reposes** dans le salon. X

4 Nous nous **regarde** dans la glace**. X

5 Vous vous **installer** à table. X

* feux *m.pl.* traffic lights ** glace *f.* ice cream; mirror

79

Exercice 14.14

Listen while you follow the text.

Before you hear the audio, look at these examples. They are explained fully in the grammar section that follows this exercise.

Tu la montres à maman.   You show **it** (*f.*) to maman.

Oui, je les vois.   Yes I see **them**.

La boîte en argent (suite) – The Silver Box (2)

C'est le soir. Toute la famille sort de table. On se repose dans le salon.

Magali.	Papa, la boîte est propre, maintenant.
Papa.	Quelle boîte?
Magali.	La petite boîte en argent. Regarde. Il y a des initiales.
Papa.	Fais voir. Ah oui … J-P. L. Qui c'est?
Magali.	Je ne sais pas.
Papa.	C'est peut-être un ancien habitant du village.
Magali.	Ou de la maison de Mme Demailly.
Papa.	Tu la montres à maman.
Magali.	Pourquoi?
Papa.	Elle s'intéresse aux antiquités.
Magali.	Maman, tu dors?
Maman.	Oh zut!
Magali.	Tu es bien réveillée maintenant?
Maman.	Mais oui, chérie. Qu'est-ce qu'il y a?
Magali.	La boîte en argent. Regarde!
Maman.	Elle est belle.
Magali.	Il y a des initiales.
Maman.	Oui, je les vois: J-P. L. Jean-Paul? Jean-Pierre?
Papa.	Il faut parler à Mamie.
Maman.	Bonne idée!

propre	clean	un habitant	an inhabitant
quelle boîte	which box?	ancien (before noun)	former
quel ...?	which ...? (*m.*)	s'intéresser à	to be interested in
quelle ...?	which ...? (*f.*)	se réveiller	to wake up
quels ...?	which ...? (*m. pl.*)	réveillé(e)	awake
quelles ...?	which ...? (*f. pl.*)	Mamie	Grandma; Granny
peut-être	perhaps	sortir de table	to leave the table

⬭ Direct object pronouns `Level 2`

Look at Exercice 14.14 again.

Notice how papa says: 'You show **it** ...' and how maman says: 'I see **them**.'

Here's a reminder:

Tu la montres

Je les vois

Let's focus on what's happening. Here, the words 'it' and 'them' (la and les) are objects of the verb.

> Reminder: The subject does the action of the verb, the object has the action of the verb done to it.

In the sentence Tu la montres, la (it, *f.*) takes the place of la boîte, so we don't have to repeat it.

In Oui, je les vois, les (them) replaces les initiales.

Because somebody is showing the box, the word 'box' (la boîte) is the object.

Because somebody is seeing the initials, the word 'initials' (les initiales) is the object.

The person or people doing the *showing* or *seeing* (verbs) are called subjects. You have used subject pronouns for a long time. They are words like je, tu, il, elle, on and so on.

Marc attaque Stéphane: sujet – Marc, verbe – attaque, objet – Stéphane

Subject pronouns		Direct object pronouns	
il	he; it	le (l')	him; it
elle	she; it	la (l')	her; it
ils	they	les	them

Finally, and very importantly, notice that the position of the object pronoun is **before the verb**, for example:

Je le vois.	I see him/it.	Tu les trouves.	You find them.
Nous l'avons.	We have it.	Elle la connaît.	She knows her.

Exercice 14.15

Complete each sentence with the right pronoun. Translate your answers into English.

1	Maman … voit.	them
2	Georges … montre à maman.	it (*f.*)
3	Papa … regarde.	them
4	Christine … veut.	it (*m.*)
5	Martine et papa … mangent.	it (*m.*)
6	M. Simonneau … trouve.	her
7	Le prof … lit.	it (*m.*)
8	Les enfants … écoutent.	him
9	Marie-Claire … quitte.	it (*m.*)
10	Zazie … aime.	them

Exercice 14.16

Write these sentences with pronouns instead of the words in **bold**. Again, take care with the **position** of the pronoun, for example:

Je mange le poisson – Je le **mange.**

1 Paul et Philippe regardent le **film.**

2 Jacqueline nettoie la **voiture.**

3 Claire aime le **bœuf.**

4 Pauline préfère les **frites.**

5 Moi, j'adore les **fruits de mer.**

Some extra questions if you have time to spare:

6 Maman commande la **truite***.

7 Pierre écoute le **professeur.**

8 Le prof raconte l'**histoire** (*f.*).

9 Tu veux le **livre**?

10 Oui, je veux le **livre.**

* truite (*f.*)   trout

Exercice 14.17

Work in pairs. The first person (A) reads out the question, then the second (B) answers with a pronoun, for example:

A. Tu vois le cinéma?   **You see the cinema?**

B. Oui, je le vois.   **Yes, I see it.**

Here are A's parts:

1 Tu vois le bateau?

2 Tu manges la banane?

3 Tu regardes le film?

4 Tu aimes les bandes dessinées?

5 Tu touches la table?

Exam style   Exercice 14.18

Presentation

Mon restaurant préféré ou La cuisine que j'aime

Prepare a short presentation **either** on your favourite restaurant **or** the style of cooking that you like best. Try to speak for about half a minute.

Expressions you may find useful:

Bonjour, je m'appelle …	Hello, my name is …
Je vais parler de …	I'm going to speak about …
J'habite à …	I live in …
Je mange (quelquefois/souvent) au restaurant	I (sometimes/often) eat out
À … il y a un restaurant …	In … there's a restaurant …
La cuisine (…) est spéciale. Par exemple, …	The cooking is different. For example, …
Un plat classique, c'est …	A typical dish is …

15 Chez le médecin

In this chapter, you will learn how to speak and write about feeling ill, accidents, injuries, mishaps and going to the doctor's. You learn how to tell people what to do and more about the negative.

Exercice 15.1

80

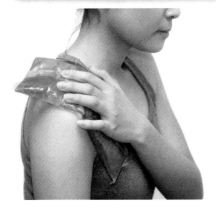

Study the vocabulary before you listen to the audio, then attempt the questions that follow.

aïe!	ouch!	téléphoner	to phone
ça fait mal	that/it hurts!	ne … rien	nothing
qu'est-ce qu'il y a?	what's the matter?	avoir de la chance	to be lucky
avoir mal à	to have pain in	casser	to break
l'épaule (f.)	the shoulder	le bras cassé	the/a broken arm
le médecin	the doctor	faire mal	to hurt
au fait	by the way	demander à	to ask (someone)
jouer du violon	to play the violin	la vie	life
aux urgences	in A&E	depuis	since

Answer in English.

1 What is wrong with Mme Demailly?

2 Why?

3 What is she going to do about it?

4 What happened to papa while cycling?

5 What happened to Magali's friend?

Exercice 15.2

Using the vocabulary and what you heard on the audio for Exercice 15.1, translate the following.

1 My arm hurts/I have pain in the arm   avoir mal, bras (*m.*)

2 It's the music, it's not serious   musique (*f.*), grave

3 My friend has a broken arm   copain (*m.*), cassé

Les parties du corps – Parts of the body

We are talking about the cheerful subject of accidents, illnesses, injuries, mishaps and going to the doctor's, so it's time to revise parts of the body!

Learn the parts of the body – les parties du corps – from this diagram:

les cheveux — l'œil — le doigt — l'oreille — le coude — la figure, le visage

la tête — la main — le pouce — le nez — la bouche — l'épaule — le bras — le cou

le dos — la poitrine — la taille — le ventre

le genou

la jambe

le pied

It is a good idea to split them in your mind into masculine and feminine words:

Les mots masculins		Les mots féminins	
le bras	the arm	la bouche	the mouth
le cou	the neck	la gorge	the throat
le coude	the elbow	la dent	the tooth
le doigt	the finger	la figure	the face
le dos	the back	la jambe	the leg
le genou	the knee	la main	the hand
le nez	the nose	la poitrine	the chest
le pied	the foot	la tête	the head
le pouce	the thumb	la taille	the waist
le ventre	the tummy	la peau	the skin

A few parts of the body begin with vowels:

l'œil (*m.*) (plural: **les** yeux)	the eye
l'oreille (*f.*)	the ear
l'épaule (*f.*)	the shoulder

And a noun that is always plural:

| les cheveux (*m.*) | the hair |

◯ Avoir mal (another avoir idiom)

M. Simonneau is complaining about **having pain** in his back.

In English, there are other ways to express this:

My back hurts.   I have backache.

Avoir mal is followed by à, which means you have to think of au and the other ways of saying 'to the'. Here are a few examples that will serve as a quick reminder:

J'ai mal au dos.

I have pain **in the** back.

My back hurts.

J'ai mal à la tête.

I have pain **in the** head.

I have a headache.

Elle a mal à l'épaule.

She has pain **in the** shoulder.

Her shoulder hurts.

Il a mal à la main.

He has pain **in the** hand.

His hand hurts.

Exam style | Exercice 15.3

Write out the sentences in full, for example:

Je + avoir mal + tête. – J'ai mal à la tête.

Check the gender of any words in Les parties du corps.

1 Je + avoir mal + main.

2 Tu + avoir mal + épaule.

3 Il + avoir mal + jambes.

4 Vous + avoir mal + bras?

5 Je + avoir mal + ventre.

Time to spare? Try these extra questions.

6 Elle + avoir mal + tête.

7 Tu + avoir mal + gorge?

8 Non, je + avoir mal + dents.

9 M. Duval + avoir mal + nez.

10 Valérie + avoir mal + cou.

Chez le médecin – At the doctor's

A note about going to the doctor in France:

First of all, there are two words for a doctor: le médecin and le docteur.

They are people, not places, so 'to the doctor' is chez le médecin, not au médecin.

Next, making an appointment is easy, as long as you know what to expect to hear on the phone. You'll spot all the standard phrases as you work through the dialogues and exercises that follow.

Finally, when you have explained what is wrong, the doctor will tell you what to do, so we are going to learn about how to do commands in French – l'impératif.

Exercice 15.4

81

Listen as you read the dialogue.

Mme Demailly prend rendez-vous.

(Elle compose le numéro de téléphone du docteur.)

Réceptionniste.	Cabinet du docteur Flaubert, bonjour.
Mme Demailly.	Ah oui. Bonjour, madame. Je voudrais prendre rendez-vous avec le docteur Flaubert.
Réceptionniste.	Oui, madame. Vous êtes Madame …?
Mme Demailly.	Demailly: D E M A I L L Y

Réceptionniste.	Quel jour voulez-vous venir?
Mme Demailly.	Demain, si possible, vers onze heures.
Réceptionniste.	D'accord, demain, mardi, à …10 h 45? Ça va?
Mme Demailly.	C'est parfait.
Réceptionniste.	Bon. À mardi 5 septembre à 10 h 45. C'est noté!
Mme Demailly.	Merci, madame. Au revoir.
Réceptionniste.	Merci. À demain. Au revoir.

composer un numéro	to dial a number
chez	to/at the house of; to/at the workplace of
prendre rendez-vous	to make an appointment
le cabinet	doctor's surgery
vers	towards
parfait	perfect
c'est noté	it's written down

Work in pairs. Practise and perform the conversation above. Take these parts:

A. Réceptionniste au cabinet du docteur Camus

B. Client/e 1. Monsieur ou Madame Blanchard

A. Réceptionniste au cabinet du docteur Beauvoir

B. Client/e 2: Monsieur ou Madame Colbert

Exercice 15.5

82

Read the text as you listen to the audio track.

Dans le cabinet du docteur Flaubert.

Dr Flaubert.	Mme Demailly?
Mme Demailly.	C'est moi, oui.
Dr Flaubert.	Bonjour, Madame Demailly; entrez. Alors, qu'est-ce qui ne va pas?
Mme Demailly.	C'est mon épaule, docteur. J'ai très mal à l'épaule.
Dr Flaubert.	Ah bon! Allongez-vous là. On va regarder cela. Ça vous fait mal … là?
Mme Demailly.	Non …
Dr Flaubert.	Et … là?

Mme Demailly.	Aïe! Eh oui, ça fait très mal!
Dr Flaubert.	Vous jouez toujours du violon?
Mme Demailly.	Oui. Je fais beaucoup de musique en ce moment.
Dr Flaubert.	Ça ne m'étonne pas. Je vais vous donner une ordonnance. Allez à la pharmacie Maurice, rue de la République. Achetez cette crème. Mettez de la crème sur votre épaule, deux fois par jour.
Mme Demailly.	Merci, docteur. Au revoir.
Dr Flaubert.	Au revoir, madame.

qu'est-ce qui ne va pas?	what is wrong?
allongez-vous	lie down
s'allonger	to lie down
faire mal à	to hurt; to cause pain to
aïe!	ouch!
étonner	to surprise
ça ne m'étonne pas	it doesn't surprise me
une ordonnance	a prescription
une crème	a cream
la pharmacie	the pharmacy; the chemist's shop
la rue	the street

The imperative – Telling people what to do

As you have probably noticed, telling each other what to do is pretty much the same in French as it is in English:

Buy this cream!	**Achetez** cette crème!
Put some cream on your back!	**Mettez** de la crème sur votre dos!

To form the imperative, we simply take the 'you' form, singular or plural (depending on whom we are talking to), with one small exception: if the last vowel of the singular form is an e or an a, which it normally is, leave off the s.

Here are a few examples:

Tu manges	**Mange** ton sandwich!	Eat your sandwich!
Tu touches	**Touche** ta tête!	Touch your head!
Tu ouvres	**Ouvre** la fenêtre!	Open the window!
Tu vas à Paris	**Va** à Paris!	Go to Paris!

However, where the last vowel is an i, keep the s:

Tu lis un livre	**Lis** un livre!	Read a book!
Tu finis ton journal	**Finis** ton journal!	Finish your newspaper!

We can also encourage **each other** to do things:

Mangeons!	Let's eat!	Rentrons!	Let's go home!

Here is one irregular command, but you do hear it quite often!

Sois sage!/Soyez sages!   Be good! (from être, 'to be')

And a couple that will be familiar:

Assieds-toi!	Sit down! (*sing.*)	Asseyez-vous!	Sit down! (*pl.*)

Here are a few others you will come across:

Allonge-toi!/Allongez-vous!	Lie down!; Stretch out! (from s'allonger)
Lève-toi!/Levez-vous!	Get up! (from se lever)
Mets-toi là!/Mettez-vous là!	Go over there! (from se mettre)
Couche-toi!/Couchez-vous!	Lie down! (from se coucher)

Exam style   Exercice 15.6

Level 2

Role play: Chez le médecin

Work in pairs. Take it in turns to be the patient (A) and the doctor (B). B begins.

A.	B.
	Bonjour, entrez!
Hello Doctor.	Qu'est-ce qui ne va pas?
My back hurts.	Allongez-vous là. Ça vous fait mal là?
Yes, it hurts!	Voici une ordonnance.
What is it for? ('It is for what?')	C'est pour une crème.
Where is the pharmacy?	Rue Lepic, derrière l'église.
Thank you. How much is it?	Vingt-cinq euros, s'il vous plaît.

Exercice 15.7

You're in charge. Tell your partner to do these things. Look at the example first:

regarder la télévision – Regarde la télévision!

1 donner ta trousse

2 fermer la fenêtre

3 toucher le plancher/le plafond

4 écrire au tableau

5 ouvrir la porte

Exercice 15.8

83

La boîte en argent (suite) – The Silver Box (3)
Read the conversation as you listen to the audio:

C'est le lendemain. Magali et Chloé quittent la maison pour aller chez leur grand-mère.

Magali.　　C'est quand, la dernière fois chez Mamie?

Chloé.　　Bof. Je ne sais pas. Avant les vacances.

Magali.　　Tu as raison. Elle va dire …

Chloé.　　… que nous ne venons jamais!

Magali.　　Oui! Mais ce n'est pas drôle, à son âge.

Chloé.　　Non. Elle a quatre-vingt-cinq ans: elle a du mal à sortir.

Magali.　　Elle ne sort jamais, elle ne voit personne, elle ne fait rien.

Chloé.　　Si! Elle fait la cuisine, elle lit, elle écrit des lettres …

la dernière fois	the last time	ne … personne	no one
avant	before	ne … rien	nothing
avoir raison	to be right	drôle	funny
avoir du mal à (+ *infin.*)	to find it hard to …	leur(s)	their
ne … jamais	never		

Correct the mistakes in **bold**.

1 The children last saw their grandmother **last week.**

2 Mamie is **fifty-five.**

3 She goes out **every day.**

4 She can only **play tennis and football.**

145

More about negative expressions

Earlier on, you learned all about the simple negative – saying 'not' – using ne and pas. In the dialogue above, there are three more negative expressions: one you've seen before and two new ones. They are used in a similar way to ne ... pas: ne before the verb and a word in place of pas after:

ne ... rien	Je ne vois rien	I see nothing; I don't see anything
ne ... jamais	Elle ne parle jamais	She never speaks; She doesn't ever speak
ne ... personne	Tu ne trouves personne	You find no one; You don't find anyone

Do not use pas as well as the words rien, jamais and personne. These words are used *instead* of pas.

Note that rien and personne can actually be used as *subjects* of verbs:

Rien n'arrive   **Nothing** happens   Personne ne sait   **Nobody** knows

Again, notice how pas is not used in these phrases.

Exam style | Exercice 15.9

84

Study the vocabulary before you listen to the audio, then answer the questions in English.

vous voici!	here you are!	toutes les semaines	every week
un grincement	a creaking; a squeaking	il vient	he comes
me dit	says to me; tells me	quelque chose	something
trop de	too many; too much	un trésor	a treasure

Correct the mistakes in **bold**:

1 Papa **sent an email** to let Mamie know the children were coming.

2 Today, she has **a bad foot and a headache.**

3 She writes with her **right hand.**

◯ Les verbes: venir and tenir

venir: to come		tenir: to hold	
je vien**s**	nous ven**ons**	je tien**s**	nous ten**ons**
tu vien**s**	vous ven**ez**	tu tien**s**	vous ten**ez**
il vien**t**	ils vien**nent**	il tien**t**	ils tien**nent**
elle vien**t**	elles vien**nent**	elle tien**t**	elles tien**nent**

Exam style — Exercice 15.10

85

Listen to the passage. Then in small doses, read it out loud to practise your accent.

Magali commence à raconter l'histoire de la boîte en argent. Elle montre la boîte à Mamie. Elle dit qu'on ne connaît pas l'identité de son propriétaire. Mamie prend ses vieilles lunettes et les met sur son nez. Elle regarde les initiales J-P. L. Elle ne les reconnaît pas. Mais soudain, elle s'arrête. Elle lève les yeux, regarde droit devant elle et dit, d'un ton mystérieux:
«Je me demande …» Mamie se lève et passe dans la salle à manger, où elle commence à feuilleter un vieil album de photos. Chloé boit son coca en silence. Elle regarde sa sœur. Magali regarde la boîte.

on ne connaît pas	one does not know (*i.e.* 'nobody knows')	droit devant elle	straight ahead of her
raconter l'histoire	to tell the story	d'un ton mystérieux	in a mysterious tone (of voice)
le/la propriétaire	the owner	feuilleter	to flip through pages
les lunettes (*f.*)	the glasses (spectacles)	un vieil album de photos	an old photo album
lever les yeux	to look up (*literally* 'to raise the eyes')		

Vrai ou faux?

1 Chloé raconte l'histoire de la boîte à Mamie.

2 Mamie a du mal à voir et à lire.

3 Au début, elle ne connaît pas l'identité de «J-P. L.»

4 Mamie quitte la cuisine.

Exercice 15.11

Translate into English.

1 Magali commence à raconter l'histoire.
2 Elle dit que Chloé boit du coca.
3 Magali montre la boîte à Mamie.
4 Mamie prend ses lunettes.
5 Soudain, elle s'arrête.

6 Elle regarde les initiales.
7 La grand-mère se lève.
8 Je me demande.
9 Chloé boit son coca.
10 Magali se demande.

Exercice 15.12

Find the odd one out in each list and say why, for example:

1 jambe: **It's a part of the body (in a list of fruits)**

Here are the categories:

1 les fruits
2 les articles de classe
3 les vêtements
4 les parties du corps
5 les sports
6 les couleurs

1	2	3	4	5	6
tomate	cahier	chemise	pied	tennis	bras
banane	crayon	cravate	brun	natation	violet
fraise	pomme	voile	coude	gomme	noir
jambe	règle	pantalon	épaule	escalade	rouge
poire	stylo	chaussure	main	football	vert

Exam style Exercice 15.13

Read this paragraph. Imagine that the information in it applies to you.

Tu es en vacances chez un(e) ami(e) à Nice. Lundi, tu es malade. Mardi, tu vas chez le médecin, qui te donne une ordonnance. Tu vas à la pharmacie et tu achètes des comprimés et du sirop. Maintenant, ça va bien. Il fait beau et tu vas jouer au tennis cet après-midi.

Answer the following questions.

1 Where are you staying in Nice?
2 When are you ill?
3 Where do you go on Tuesday?

4 What do you buy there?
5 What are you going to do this afternoon?

Exam style | Exercice 15.14

86

Listen as you read then do the exercises.

Tochiko va à la pharmacie en ville. Elle doit faire des achats pour toute la famille.

Elle entre dans le magasin.

La pharmacienne.	Bonjour, mademoiselle. Ça va?
Tochiko.	Bonjour, madame. Ça va très bien, merci. Mais j'ai chaud!
La pharmacienne.	Ah oui. Il fait chaud aujourd'hui. Mais c'est la fin de l'été. Alors …
Tochiko.	Alors aujourd'hui, il me faut … attendez, j'ai une liste.
La pharmacienne.	Je vous écoute!
Tochiko.	Je voudrais du dentifrice pour Marie-Christine, une brosse à dents pour maman, des pastilles pour Pascal, Mina veut du shampooing, et pour moi du savon et un peigne. Et puis les comprimés de grand-père aussi, s'il vous plaît.
La pharmacienne.	Vous avez l'ordonnance?
Tochiko.	Oui! La voici. Tenez.

le/la pharmacien/ne	the pharmacist, chemist	le shampooing	the shampoo
la fin	the end (time)	le savon	the soap
il me faut	I need	le peigne	the comb
le dentifrice	the toothpaste	le comprimé	the pill
des pastilles	throat sweets		

1 Answer in English.

   (a) How is Tochiko feeling today?

   (b) What time of year is it?

   (c) How does Tochiko remember what to get at the chemist's?

   (d) What does she want for herself?

   (e) What does she need for her grandfather's pills?

2 Practise and perform the dialogue above in class.

G Grammar

◯ Where to look things up

Grammar summary

1 You – How to choose the right word for 'you'

tu   is for a young person of your age, a member of your family or a pet.

vous   is for any adult you don't know well (a teacher, shopkeeper, etc.) or for more than one person.

Adults use vous for speaking to another adult until they know him or her well.

2 The – How to say 'the'

le	is for a masculine noun in the singular	le disque
la	is for a feminine noun in the singular	la radio
l'	is for a singular noun beginning with a vowel or a silent 'h' except some words (the dictionary tells you which ones), which keep le or la	l'école, l'hôtel la haie*, le héros*
les	is for all plural nouns	les vélos

* la haie = the hedge; le héros = the hero.

In these words, we do not pronounce the 'h' in the English way, but the words are treated in every other way as though we did.

3 A (an) – How to say 'a'

un   is for a masculine noun   un hôtel

une is for a feminine noun   une forêt

4 Some/any – How to say 'some' or 'any'

du	is for a masculine noun in the singular	du lait
de la	is for a feminine noun in the singular	de la salade
de l'	is for a singular noun beginning with a vowel or silent 'h'	de l'argent
des	is for all plural nouns	des oranges

Note that in English we often leave out the word 'some'; it is never left out in French:

e.g. You have (some) books and pencils. = Tu as des livres et des crayons.

5   Plurals – How to make nouns plural

To make a noun plural, we usually just add -s:	un livre, des livres
Nouns ending in -eau add -x:	un cadeau, des cadeaux
Most nouns ending in -al generally change -al to -aux:	un cheval, des chevaux

6   My – Choosing the right word for 'my'

'My' followed by a masculine singular noun is mon:

mon livre = my book

'My' followed by a feminine singular noun is usually ma:

ma sœur = my sister

However, 'my' followed by a feminine noun beginning with a vowel or silent 'h' is mon:

mon amie = my friend (*f.*)

'My' followed by any plural noun is mes:

mes livres = my books

7   Your (when using tu) – How to choose the right word for 'your'

The words for 'your', ton, ta, tes, work in exactly the same way as mon, ma, mes:

ton livre = your book

ta sœur = your sister, but ton amie = your friend (*f.*)

tes livres = your books

The word for 'your' followed by a feminine noun beginning with a vowel or a silent 'h' is ton:

ton amie = your friend (*f.*).

8   His/her and their – How to choose the right word

The word for 'his' and 'her' is the same in French, regardless of whether the 'owner' is male or female:

When followed by a masculine noun, it is son:

son livre = his/her book.

The word for 'his' or 'her' followed by a feminine noun is sa:

sa sœur = his/her sister.

The word for 'his' or 'her' with a plural noun is ses:

ses parents = his/her parents.

The word for 'his' or 'her' followed by a feminine noun beginning with a vowel or a silent 'h' is son:

son amie = his/her friend (*f.*).

The word for 'their' is leur (singular) and leurs (plural). It is the same for masculine and feminine nouns:

f.: leur bicyclette = their bicycle	leurs bicyclettes = their bicycles
m.: leur garage = their garage	leurs garages = their garages

9 Your (when using vous) – How to choose the right word for 'your'

votre with a singular noun, either masculine or feminine, e.g. votre vélo

vos   with a plural noun, e.g. vos vélos

10 Here is, there is – How to say 'here is/are' and 'there is/are'

When pointing to things:

voici   here is/here are

voilà   there is/there are (N.B. voilà! also means: 'there you are!')

e.g. Voilà un chien. = There is a dog (over there).

But when giving information:

il y a there is/there are

e.g. Il y a un chien dans le jardin. = There is a dog in the garden.

e.g. Il y a des araignées dans ma chambre. = There are spiders in my bedroom.

11 How to say 'not' – Basic negative and other negative expressions

Put ne before the verb and pas after it:

Je ne sais pas = I do **not** know/I do**n't** know

If there is an infinitive, put ne and pas around the verb *before* the infinitive:

Je ne vais pas chanter = I am **not** going to sing

More negative expressions:

ne … plus	no longer, not any longer, no more
ne … jamais	never, not ever
ne … rien	nothing, not anything
ne … personne	no one, not anyone

Most of these negative expressions are used in the same way as ne … pas:

Je ne mange plus de bananes.	I no longer eat bananas.
Elle ne va jamais au cinéma.	She never goes to the cinema.
On ne porte ni jeans ni baskets ici.	We don't wear jeans or trainers here.

> Reminder: In a sentence involving a plural noun, ne … que (= only), which is not really a negative expression, is followed by des.

Example:

Maman n'achète que des fruits.	Mum only buys fruit.

Personne and rien may be used as the subject of a sentence. Note the word order:

Personne ne vient me voir.	No one comes to see me.
Rien n'arrive ici.	Nothing happens here.

With formations using the infinitive, only the verb preceding the infinitive is made negative:

On ne va plus aller au parc.	We're not going to go to the park any more.

12   Adjectives – All you need to know about adjectives

Adjectives are 'describing' words. In French, they must agree with the noun they describe. Most are put *after* the noun.

The basic adjective is masculine singular	un crayon vert
To make it feminine, you normally just add an -e	une table verte
To make it plural, you normally just add an -s	des crayons verts
To make it feminine plural, add BOTH -e and -s	des tables vertes

Some have their own special (irregular) forms:

Masculine	Masculine + vowel	Feminine	Plural
beau	bel	belle	beaux/belles
nouveau	nouvel	nouvelle	nouveaux/ nouvelles
blanc		blanche	blancs/ blanches
vieux	vieil	vieille	vieux/vieilles
doux		douce	doux/douces

Note also:

gentil	gentille
bon	bonne
actif	active

Note that several adjectives come before the noun. To help you remember which, remember BAGS:

Examples:

B	Beauty	beau, joli, vilain
A	Age	jeune, vieux
G	Goodness	bon, mauvais, méchant
S	Size	grand, petit, haut, gros

Adjectives describing any of these usually go before the noun.

13   Questions – How to make questions

There are 3 ways to ask a question:

1 Reverse the order of person and verb (inversion)
2 Put Est-ce que... before the sentence, without changing anything else
3 Use your tone of voice (intonation).

Examples:

Veux-tu un bonbon?

Est-ce que tu veux un bonbon?

Tu veux un bonbon?

Questions words: a reminder

qui?	who?
que?	what?
qu'est-ce que?	what? (+ verb expression, e.g. what are you doing?)
comment?	how?
quand?	when?
pourquoi?	why?
où?	where?
combien (de)?	how many? how much?
quel, quelle, quels, quelles (+ noun)?	which …? what …?

Attention! qui is never shortened, but que becomes qu' before a vowel or silent 'h'.

14   To/at + the; of/from + the – How to say 'to', 'at', 'of' and 'from' with 'the'

We do NOT say   à le **or** à les,   de le **or** de les

Instead we say   au   aux   du   des

(a) à can mean 'to' or 'at'. To say 'to the…' or 'to/at the…':

m.	au cinéma = to/at the cinema
f.	à la piscine = to/at the swimming pool
vowel or silent 'h'	à l'homme = to the man; à l'école = to/at (the) school

The French for 'to the' or 'at the', followed by any plural noun, is aux:

aux magasins = to/at the shops

(b) de can mean 'of' or 'from'. To say 'of the…' or 'from the…':

m.	du cinéma = of/from the cinema
f.	de la piscine = of/from the swimming pool
vowel or silent 'h'	de l'homme = of/from the man; de l'école = of/from (the) school

The French for 'of the' or 'from the', followed by any plural noun, is des:

des magasins = of the shops/from the shops

15 Going to do – The future tense, using aller + infinitive
To talk about things that are going to happen, use the present tense of aller, then add the infinitive of whatever is going to happen:

je vais vendre = I am going to sell

16 Activities – Choosing between aller, faire and jouer
The French for 'to play' is jouer. Jouer is regularly followed by au:

jouer au tennis = to play tennis

jouer au ping-pong = to play table tennis

The French for 'to go' is aller:

aller à la pêche = to go fishing

However, for several activities where in English we use the verb 'to go', in French the verb faire is used:

faire du cheval = to go riding   faire du ski = to go skiing

faire un pique-nique = to go   faire une promenade = to go
for a picnic   for a walk

17 Prepositions – Position words
A preposition is a word that tells us where something is in relation to something else:

dans = in   à droite de = to the right of

derrière = behind   sur = on

devant = in front of   sous = under

à côté de = beside, next to   entre = between

à gauche de = to the left of   en face de = opposite

18 Joining words – Conjunctions
A conjunction is a word that links ideas together in a sentence:

mais = but   parce que = because

si = if   car = for, because

et = and   ou = or

19 Time and weather – Talking about time and weather

Weather

Many weather expressions use the verb faire:

Il fait beau. = It's fine.

Il fait chaud. = It is hot.

There are other weather verbs:

infinitif	présent
neiger (to snow, to be snowing)	il neige
pleuvoir (to rain, to be raining)	il pleut
geler (to freeze, to be freezing)	il gèle

Asking about the weather:

Quel temps fait-il? = What is the weather like?

Time

For telling the time we use the 24-hour clock, and il est for 'it is'.

What's the time?/What time is it?	Quelle heure est-il?
It's three o'clock	Il est trois heures
It's three in the afternoon/3 p.m.	Il est quinze heures/15 h
It's ten past five/5.10	Il est cinq heures dix/5 h 10
It's a quarter past three/3.15	Il est trois heures et quart
It's half past two/2.30	Il est deux heures et demie
It's twenty to eleven	Il est onze heures moins vingt
It's a quarter to eleven	Il est onze heures moins le quart
It's ten to eleven	Il est onze heures moins dix
It's midday/12 p.m.	Il est midi/12 h
It's midnight/12 a.m.	Il est minuit/24 h

20 To and in + place – How to say 'to' or 'in' with towns, cities and countries

Towns

For all cities, towns or villages, of any size, use à:

à Paris = to Paris; in Paris

Countries

For countries with feminine names (mostly those ending in e), use en:

en France = to France; in France

For countries with masculine names, use au:

au Canada = to Canada; in Canada

au Maroc = to Morocco; in Morocco

au Japon = to Japan; in Japan

au Portugal = to Portugal; in Portugal

au Sénégal = to Senegal; in Senegal

Countries with plural names take aux:

aux États-Unis = to the USA; in the USA

21 This/that + thing/person – How to say 'this', 'that', 'these', and 'those'

All the singular words mean *this* or *that*. The plural means *these* or *those*:

	singular	plural
m.	ce	ces
m. (before a vowel or silent 'h')	cet	ces
f.	cette	ces

22 Avoir idioms – Expressions with avoir

Avoir is used in many French expressions where English uses the verb 'to be':

avoir l'air - to seem; to appear to be

avoir besoin de = to need

avoir chaud = to be hot

avoir envie de = to want

avoir faim = to be hungry

avoir froid = to be cold

avoir honte = to be ashamed

avoir lieu = to take place

avoir peur = to be afraid

avoir raison = to be right

avoir soif = to be thirsty

avoir sommeil = to be sleepy

avoir tort = to be wrong

23 Pronouns – Words we use to avoid repeating nouns

subject (I, etc.)	direct object (me, etc.)	reflexive (myself, etc.)
je	me	me
tu	te	te
il	le	se
elle	la	se
on		se
nous	nous	nous
vous	vous	vous
ils	les	se
elles	les	se

Some special pronouns are used alone or after a preposition, as in this example in English:

A   Who had salad for lunch?

B   Me!

And in French:

A   Qui a mangé les croissants?

B   Moi!

Here are all the special (so-called 'strong') pronouns:

moi   **me**

toi   **you** (*sing.*)

lui   him

elle   her

nous   us

vous   you (*pl.*)

eux   them (*m.*)

elles   them (*f.*)

24 Imperatives (commands) – Telling people what to do

To make the 'command' form of a verb, take either the second person singular or second person plural of the verb, removing tu or vous:

Tu descends. = You go down.   >   Descends! = Go down!

Vous descendez.   >   Descendez!

On -ER verbs, remove the -s from the second person singular ending:

Tu parles. = You are speaking.   >   Parle! = Speak!

Commands using reflexive ('selfie') verbs

Do the same as for a normal verb (see above) but add -toi or -vous as appropriate:

Tu te lèves. = You get up.   >   Lève-toi! = Get up!

Vous vous levez.   >   Levez-vous!

25 Adverbs – All you need to know about adverbs

Usually an adverb is formed by adding the suffix -ment to the corresponding adjective, rather like adding -ly to 'quick' to make 'quickly' in English:

vrai   (true)   vraiment   (truly, really)

facile   (easy)   facilement   (easily)

There needs to be a vowel before -ment, so, if there isn't, use the feminine adjective:

lent   (slow)   lentement   (slowly)

Some commonly used adverbs are irregular and not formed in this way:

bientôt	soon	encore	again
quelquefois	sometimes	peu	little, not much
souvent	often	toujours	always
pire	worse		

26 That – Choosing the right word for 'that'

When trying to find the right French word for 'that', consider these examples:

That house is small   Cette maison est petite (from ce, cet, cette, ces)

Do you see that?   Tu vois ça?   (ça = it or that)

He says that Paul is French Il dit que Paul est français

Stop to think which example is the one you need.

27 Which – Choosing the right word for 'which'

When trying to find the right French word for 'which', consider these examples:

Which film are you going to see?   Tu vas voir **quel** film? (from quel, quels, quelle, quelles)

The book which you like   Le livre **que** tu aimes   (referring to the noun before *it*)

Stop to think which example is the one you need.

28 Who – Choosing the right word for 'who'

When trying to find the right French word for 'who', consider these examples:

Who has the answer?   Qui a la réponse?   (question word)

The girl who lives here   La fille **qui** habite ici   (subject of verb)

The man who(m) I know   L'homme **que** je connais   (object of verb)

Stop to think which example is the one you need.

29 Verbs

How to form each tense:

Present tense

Elle regarde. = She watches./She is watching.

(also: 'she does watch', though this is more often used in English in the negative: Elle ne regarde pas = she does not watch)

The present tenses of regular verbs are shown in tables below. Regular verbs follow patterns of stem + ending, but each irregular verb must be learnt individually from the verb tables that follow this section.

Reflexive ('selfie') verbs

Reflexive verbs are verbs that you 'do to yourself', like taking a 'selfie'.

They are the same as normal verbs, except that you have to put a 'self' word before the verb:

Elle regarde. = She looks.   Elle se regarde. = She looks at herself (e.g. in the mirror).

The 'self' words are:

me	myself	nous	ourselves
te	yourself	vous	yourself/yourselves
se	himself	se	themselves (*m.* or *f.*)
se	herself		
se	oneself		

Example: nous nous lavons = we wash ourselves

The near future (le futur proche)

This tense is made by adding the present tense of aller to an infinitive:

On va arriver. = We are going to arrive.

Tu vas partir. = You are going to leave.

Elles vont regarder. = They are going to watch.

Conditional: the 'would' tense

The conditional tense of a verb is the one that means 'would'.

For CE, you only need to know two conditional expressions:

je voudrais   I would like (from vouloir, to want)

j'aimerais   I would like (from aimer, to like)

Examples:	Je voudrais un kilo de pommes	I would like a kilo of apples
	J'aimerais aller au cinéma	I would like to go to the cinema

Verb tables

1   Regular verbs

Present tense

All regular verbs belong to one of three groups: -ER (1st group),
-IR (2nd group) and -RE (3rd group). The endings to each verb are
different depending on which group they are in. This applies to all
tenses, but is most obvious in the present:

1st group: -ER

regarder: to watch, look at					
je	regard-e	I watch	nous	regard-ons	we watch
tu	regard-es	you watch	vous	regard-ez	you watch
il	regard-e	he watches	ils	regard-ent	they watch
elle	regard-e	she watches	elles	regard-ent	they watch

2nd group: -IR

finir: to finish					
je	fin-is	I finish	nous	fin-issons	we finish
tu	fin-is	you finish	vous	fin-issez	you finish
il	fin-it	he finishes	ils	fin-issent	they finish
elle	fin-it	she finishes	elles	fin-issent	they finish

3rd group: -RE

vendre: to sell					
je	vend-s	I sell	nous	vend-ons	we sell
tu	vend-s	you sell	vous	vend-ez	you sell
il	vend	he sells	ils	vend-ent	they sell
elle	vend	she sells	elles	vend-ent	they sell

2   Reflexive verbs

Here is a reflexive verb set out in full:

se laver: to wash (oneself)			
je me lave	I wash (myself)	nous nous lavons	we wash (ourselves)
tu te laves	you wash (yourself)	vous vous lavez	you wash (yourselves)
il se lave	he washes (himself)	ils se lavent	they wash (themselves)
elle se lave	she washes (herself)	elles se lavent	they wash (themselves)

Any verb can be made reflexive, as long as it makes sense!

Je lave le chien. = I wash the dog.

Je me lave. = I wash (myself).

Near future (le futur proche)

The futur proche is made by using the present tense of aller before an infinitive:

je vais regarder	I am going to watch	nous allons regarder	we are going to watch
tu vas regarder	you are going to watch	vous allez regarder	you are going to watch
il va regarder	he is going to watch	ils vont regarder	they are going to watch
elle va regarder	she is going to watch	elles vont regarder	they are going to watch

3   Irregular verbs

Irregular verbs are those that do not follow the patterns of the three main groups. They are often the most commonly used.

acheter: to buy (è/e)	
j'achète	nous achetons
tu achètes	vous achetez
il achète	ils achètent
elle achète	elles achètent
on achète	

aller: to go	
je vais	nous allons
tu vas	vous allez
il va	ils vont
elle va	elles vont
on va	

appeler: to call (ll/l)

j' appelle	nous appelons
tu appelles	vous appelez
il appelle	ils appellent
elle appelle	elles appellent
on appelle	

s'asseoir: to sit down

je m'assieds	nous nous asseyons
tu t'assieds	vous vous asseyez
il s'assied	ils s'asseyent
elle s'assied	elles s'asseyent
on s'assied	

avoir: to have

j'ai	nous avons
tu as	vous avez
il a	ils ont
elle a	elles ont
on a	

battre: to beat

je bats	nous battons
tu bats	vous battez
il bat	ils battent
elle bat	elles battent
on bat	

boire: to drink

je bois	nous buvons
tu bois	vous buvez
il boit	ils boivent
elle boit	elles boivent
on boit	

connaître: to know (a person, place)

je connais	nous connaissons
tu connais	vous connaissez
il connaît	ils connaissent
elle connaît	elles connaissent
on connaît	

courir: to run

je cours	nous courons
tu cours	vous courez
il court	ils courent
elle court	elles courent
on court	

croire: to believe

je crois	nous croyons
tu crois	vous croyez
il croit	ils croient
elle croit	elles croient
on croit	

devoir: to have to, to owe

je dois	nous devons
tu dois	vous devez
il doit	ils doivent
elle doit	elles doivent
on doit	

dire: to say

je dis	nous disons
tu dis	vous dites
il dit	ils disent
elle dit	elles disent
on dit	

dormir: to sleep

je dors	nous dormons
tu dors	vous dormez
il dort	ils dorment
elle dort	elles dorment
on dort	

écrire: to write

j'écris	nous écrivons
tu écris	vous écrivez
il écrit	ils écrivent
elle écrit	elles écrivent
on écrit	

envoyer: to send (i/y)

j'envoie	nous envoyons
tu envoies	vous envoyez
il envoie	ils envoient
elle envoie	elles envoient
on envoie	

essayer: to try

j'essaie	nous essayons
tu essaies	vous essayez
il essaie	ils essaient
elle essaie	elles essaient
on essaie	

être: to be

je suis	nous sommes
tu es	vous êtes
il est	ils sont
elle est	elles sont
on est	

faire: to be

je fais	nous faisons
tu fais	vous faites
il fait	ils font
elle fait	elles font
on fait	

falloir: to be necessary (impersonal, only used with il)

il faut	it is necessary to

jeter: to throw (tt/t)

je jette	nous jetons
tu jettes	vous jetez
il jette	ils jettent
elle jette	elles jettent
on jette	

lire: to read

je lis	nous lisons
tu lis	vous lisez
il lit	ils lisent
elle lit	elles lisent
on lit	

mener: to lead (è/e)

je mène	nous menons
tu mènes	vous menez
il mène	ils mènent
elle mène	elles mènent
on mène	

mettre: to put, to put on

je mets	nous mettons
tu mets	vous mettez
il met	ils mettent
elle met	elles mettent
on met	

mourir: to die

elle meurt	elles meurent
il meurt	ils meurent
je meurs	nous mourons
on meurt	vous mourez
tu meurs	

naître: to be born

je nais	nous naissons
tu nais	vous naissez
il naît	ils naissent
elle naît	elles naissent
on naît	

ouvrir: to open

j'ouvre	nous ouvrons
tu ouvres	vous ouvrez
il ouvre	ils ouvrent
elle ouvre	elles ouvrent
on ouvre	

partir: to leave

je pars	nous partons
tu pars	vous partez
il part	ils partent
elle part	elles partent
on part	

pouvoir: to be able to

je peux	nous pouvons
tu peux	vous pouvez
il peut	ils peuvent
elle peut	elles peuvent
on peut	

prendre: to take

je prends	nous prenons
tu prends	vous prenez
il prend	ils prennent
elle prend	elles prennent
on prend	

recevoir: to receive

je reçois	nous recevons
tu reçois	vous recevez
il reçoit	ils reçoivent
elle reçoit	elles reçoivent
on reçoit	

rire: to laugh

je ris	nous rions
tu ris	vous riez
il rit	ils rient
elle rit	elles rient
on rit	

savoir: to know

je sais	nous savons
tu sais	vous savez
il sait	ils savent
elle sait	elles savent
on sait	

sécher: to dry (è/é)

je sèche	nous séchons
tu sèches	vous séchez
il sèche	ils sèchent
elle sèche	elles sèchent
on sèche	

sourire: to smile

je souris	nous sourions
tu souris	vous souriez
il sourit	ils sourient
elle sourit	elles sourient
on sourit	

suivre: to follow

je suis	nous suivons
tu suis	vous suivez
il suit	ils suivent
elle suit	elles suivent
on suit	

tenir: to hold

je tiens	nous tenons
tu tiens	vous tenez
il tient	ils tiennent
elle tient	elles tiennent
on tient	

venir: to come

je viens	nous venons
tu viens	vous venez
il vient	ils viennent
elle vient	elles viennent
on vient	

vivre: to live

je vis	nous vivons
tu vis	vous vivez
il vit	ils vivent
elle vit	elles vivent
on vit	

voir: to see

je vois	nous voyons
tu vois	vous voyez
il voit	ils voient
elle voit	elles voient
on voit	

vouloir: to want

je veux	nous voulons
tu veux	vous voulez
il veut	ils veulent
elle veut	elles veulent